Lecture Notes in Computer Science 12964

More information about this subseries at http://www.springer.com/series/7412

Nandinee Haq · Patricia Johnson ·
Andreas Maier · Tobias Würfl · Jaejun Yoo (Eds.)

Machine Learning
for Medical
Image Reconstruction

4th International Workshop, MLMIR 2021
Held in Conjunction with MICCAI 2021
Strasbourg, France, October 1, 2021
Proceedings

Editors
Nandinee Haq 🆔
Sunnybrook Health Science Centre
Toronto, ON, Canada

Andreas Maier 🆔
Pattern Recognition Lab at FAU
Erlangen, Germany

Jaejun Yoo 🆔
Ulsan National Institute of Science
and Technology
Ulsan, Korea (Republic of)

Patricia Johnson 🆔
NYU Grossman School of Medicine
New York City, NY, USA

Tobias Würfl 🆔
Siemens Healthineers
Erlangen, Germany

ISSN 0302-9743   ISSN 1611-3349 (electronic)
Lecture Notes in Computer Science
ISBN 978-3-030-88551-9   ISBN 978-3-030-88552-6 (eBook)
https://doi.org/10.1007/978-3-030-88552-6

LNCS Sublibrary: SL6 – Image Processing, Computer Vision, Pattern Recognition, and Graphics

This Springer imprint is published by the registered company Springer Nature Switzerland AG
The registered company address is: Gewerbestrasse 11, 6330 Cham, Switzerland

Preface

We are proud to present the proceedings for the Fourth Workshop on Machine Learning for Medical Image Reconstruction (MLMIR 2021) which was held on October 1, 2021, online, as part of the 24nd Medical Image Computing and Computer Assisted Intervention (MICCAI 2021) conference.

Image reconstruction commonly refers to solving an inverse problem, recovering a latent image of some physical parameter from a set of noisy measurements assuming a physical model of the generating process between the image and the measurements. In medical imaging two particularly widespread applications are computed tomography (CT) and magnetic resonance imaging (MRI). Using these two modalities as examples, conditions have been established under which the associated reconstruction problems can be solved uniquely. However, in many cases there is a need to recover solutions from fewer measurements to reduce patient exposure or to reduce the measurement time. The theory of compressed sensing showed how to pursue this while still enabling accurate reconstruction by using prior knowledge about the imaged objects. A critical question is the construction of suitable models of prior knowledge about images. Research has departed from constructing explicit priors for images and moved towards learning suitable priors from large datasets using machine learning (ML).

After three previous successful workshops, we found that for applications in MR such techniques have already been incorporated into clinical products by different vendors. Therefore, the focus of the scientific community shifted to more complex applications in MR and application to other modalities. We believe that this meeting still serves a valuable place to advance the dissemination of such techniques and enable joint discussions about this direction of research.

Its cross-modality approach brings together researchers from various modalities ranging from CT and MRI to microscopy and X-ray fluoroscopy. We believe joint discussion fosters the translation of algorithms between modalities.

We were fortunate that Yonina Eldar (Weizmann Institute of Science) and Jongho Lee (Seoul National University) accepted our invitation as keynote speakers and presented fascinating keynote lectures about the state of the art in this growing field. Despite the still ongoing special circumstances of the COVID-19 pandemic, we received 20 submissions and accepted 13 papers for inclusion in the workshop. The topics of the accepted papers cover a broad range of medical image reconstruction problems. The predominant machine learning technique used for reconstruction problems continues to be deep neural networks.

September 2021

Nandinee Haq
Patricia Johnson
Andreas Maier
Tobias Würfl
Jaejun Yoo

Organization

Workshop Organizers

Nandinee Haq   Sunnybrook Research Institute, Canada
Patricia Johnson   New York University, USA
Andreas Maier   Friedrich-Alexander-University
     Erlangen-Nuremberg, Germany
Tobias Würfl   Siemens Healthineers, Germany
Jaejun Yoo   Ulsan National Institute of Science and
     Technology, South Korea

Scientific Program Committee

Delaram Behnami   University of British Columbia, Canada
Dong Bin   Peking University, China
Teodora Chitiboi   Siemens Healthineers, USA
Tolga Cukur   Bilkent University, Turkey
Farah Deeba   University of British Columbia, Canada
Bruno De Man   GE, USA
Kerstin Hammernik   Imperial College London, UK
Dong Liang   Chinese Academy of Sciences, China
Matthew Muckley   Facebook AI Research, USA
Ozan Öktem   KTH Royal Institute of Technology, Sweden
Thomas Pock   Graz University of Technology, Austria
Essam Rashed   British University in Egypt, Egypt
Bruno Riemenschneider   New York University, USA
Daniel Rückert   Technical University Munich, Germany
Ge Wang   Rensselaer Polytechnic Institute, USA
Shanshan Wang   Shenzhen Institute of Advanced Technology,
     China
Guang Yang   Royal Brompton Hospital, UK
Jong Chul Ye   KAIST, South Korea

Contents

Deep Learning for General Image Reconstruction

Deep Learning for Magnetic Resonance Imaging

HyperRecon: Regularization-Agnostic CS-MRI Reconstruction with Hypernetworks

Alan Q. Wang[1]([✉]), Adrian V. Dalca[2,3], and Mert R. Sabuncu[1]

[1] School of Electrical and Computer Engineering, Cornell University, Ithaca, USA
aw847@cornell.edu
[2] Computer Science and Artificial Intelligence Lab, Massachusetts Institute
of Technology, Cambridge, USA
[3] A.A. Martinos Center for Biomedical Imaging, Massachusetts General Hospital,
Harvard Medical School, Boston, USA

Abstract. Reconstructing under-sampled k-space measurements in Compressed Sensing MRI (CS-MRI) is classically solved by minimizing a regularized least-squares cost function. In the absence of fully-sampled training data, this optimization approach can still be amortized via a neural network that minimizes the cost function over a dataset of under-sampled measurements. Here, a crucial design choice is the regularization function(s) and corresponding weight(s). In this paper, we introduce HyperRecon – a novel strategy of using a hypernetwork to generate the parameters of a main reconstruction network as a function of the regularization weight(s), resulting in a regularization-agnostic reconstruction model. At test time, for a given under-sampled image, our model can rapidly compute reconstructions with different amounts of regularization. We propose and empirically demonstrate an efficient and data-driven way of maximizing reconstruction performance given limited hypernetwork capacity. Our code will be made publicly available upon acceptance.

Keywords: Compressed sensing MRI · Hypernetworks · Amortized optimization

1 Introduction

Compressed sensing magnetic resonance imaging (CS-MRI) is a promising direction for accelerating MRI acquisition [24] and yields a well-studied ill-posed inverse problem. Classically, this problem is solved via an optimization which minimizes a regularized regression cost function on each collected measurement set [3,4,6,9,12,38,39].

Amortized optimization extends this idea by training a neural network to minimize the cost function using large datasets. While often cited in the context of variational autoencoders [10,19,32], amortized optimization has been applied to image registration [2] and CS-MRI reconstruction [34], and has been shown

© Springer Nature Switzerland AG 2021
N. Haq et al. (Eds.): MLMIR 2021, LNCS 12964, pp. 3–13, 2021.
https://doi.org/10.1007/978-3-030-88552-6_1

to boast faster and often better performance than its classical counterparts. Additionally, in contrast to supervised neural network reconstruction methods [1,35–37], amortized optimization is performed without access to full-resolution data, which can be difficult to obtain in large quantities in the clinical setting.

Unfortunately, both the classical and amortized methods suffer from a strong dependence on the regularization function, the weighting of which can vastly affect reconstructions. In practice, considerable time and resources can be spent setting the weight(s) of regularization, using costly methods such as grid-search, random search, or Bayesian optimization [23,30,40].

Recently, hypernetworks have been proposed to automate hyperparameter tuning; the hypernetwork takes as input the hyperparameter and outputs the weights of the main network which performs the main task [5,17,22]. In this paper, we build on this idea and propose a *regularization-agnostic* strategy for CS-MRI reconstruction using amortized optimization.

Specifically, our model, which we call HyperRecon, uses a hypernetwork that takes as input a value (or values) for the regularization weight(s) and outputs the parameters of a reconstruction network which solves the amortized optimization. At test-time, arbitrary weight values can be inputted and corresponding reconstructions will be efficiently computed, leading to arbitrarily large numbers of reconstructions.

The flexibility HyperRecon offers has two important ramifications which we explore in this paper. First, rapid and automated hyperparameter tuning is now possible, drawing from a rich set of candidate values in a continuous range. Second, analyses on the diversity of reconstructions resulting from different regularization weights can be conducted; indeed, end users can view different reconstructions as easily as turning a dial. In this work, we explore both directions in the context of CS-MRI, but stress that this idea is broadly applicable to any method involving regularization hyperparameters.

Our contributions are as follows. We propose a CS-MRI reconstruction method which efficiently produces a rich variety of probable reconstructions at test-time. Additionally, we present a novel data-driven method of hyperparameter sampling during training that allows us to efficiently allocate model capacity and optimize performance. We visualize and quantify the impact of hyperparameter sampling during training on the quality and range of reconstructions, and empirically demonstrate significant improvement when data-driven sampling is used.

2   Background

2.1   Amortized Optimization of CS-MRI

In the classical CS-MRI formulation, a reconstruction of the unobserved full-resolution MRI scan[1] $x \in \mathbb{C}^N$ is obtained by solving an optimization

$$\arg \min_{x} J(x, y) + \sum_{i=1}^{p} \alpha_i \mathcal{R}_i(x) \qquad (1)$$

---

[1] In this paper, we assume a single coil acquisition.

for each under-sampled measurement $\boldsymbol{y} \in \mathbb{C}^M$, where N is the number of pixels of the full-resolution grid and $M < N$ is the number of measurements.

The data-consistency (DC) loss, which can be defined as $J(\boldsymbol{x}, \boldsymbol{y}) = \|\mathcal{F}_u \boldsymbol{x} - \boldsymbol{y}\|_2^2$ where $\mathcal{F}_u$ denotes the under-sampled Fourier operator, encourages $\boldsymbol{x}$ to be consistent with the measurement $\boldsymbol{y}$. The latter summation includes p regularization terms, $\mathcal{R}_i(\boldsymbol{x})$, each weighted by a hyperparameter $\alpha_i \in \mathbb{R}_+$ which determine the degree of trade-off between the $p+1$ competing terms. The regularization terms are engineered to restrict the solutions to the space of probable images, with common choices including sparsity-inducing norms of wavelet coefficients [13], total variation (TV) [18,29], and their combinations [24,27].

A deep-learning based extension of this idea involves solving Eq. (1) with a neural network [34]. Given a neural network G_θ parameterized with θ and a training set $\mathcal{D}$ of under-sampled measurements $\boldsymbol{y}$, the problem reduces to:

$$\arg \min_\theta \sum_{\boldsymbol{y} \in \mathcal{D}} \left[J(G_\theta(\boldsymbol{y}), \boldsymbol{y}) + \sum_{i=1}^p \alpha_i \mathcal{R}_i(G_\theta(\boldsymbol{y})) \right]. \tag{2}$$

This formulation can be viewed as an amortization of the instance-specific optimization of Eq. (1), via a neural network G_θ [10,15,25]. Amortized optimization allows for fast solving of the classical optimization with a forward pass through G_θ, while also exhibiting advantageous regularization properties [2,32]. In addition, it does not require any full-resolution data to train, unlike supervised deep learning based reconstruction techniques [1,35–37].

2.2 Hypernetworks

Originally introduced for achieving weight-sharing and model compression [16], hypernetworks take as input a set of hyperparameters that are in turn converted to the weights of the network that solves the main task, such as classification. This idea has found numerous applications including neural architecture search [5,41], Bayesian neural networks [21,33], multi-task learning [20,26,31], and hyperparameter optimization [17,22]. For example, hypernetworks have been used as a means of replacing cross-validation for finding the optimal level of weight decay on MNIST classification [22]. Similarly, in parallel work, hypernetworks were used to build a hyperparameter-invariant medical image registration framework [17].

3   Proposed Method

3.1   Regularization-Agnostic Reconstruction Network

Define a vector of regularization weights $\boldsymbol{\alpha} = [\alpha_1, \alpha_2, ..., \alpha_p]^T \in \mathbb{R}_+^p$. Let G_θ denote a main network which maps measurements $\boldsymbol{y}$ to reconstructions $\hat{\boldsymbol{x}}$, whose parameters are denoted as $\theta \in \Theta$. A hypernetwork $H_\phi : \mathbb{R}_+^p \rightarrow \Theta$ maps $\boldsymbol{\alpha}$ to the parameters θ of the main network G_θ. The model is illustrated in Fig. 1.

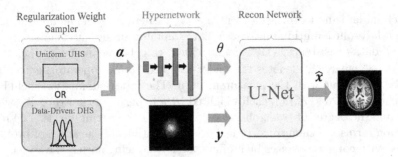

Fig. 1. Proposed model. Reconstruction network takes as input the measurement y and outputs reconstruction $\hat{x}$, while the hypernetwork takes as input the hyperparameter α and outputs weights θ for the reconstruction network. During training, α is sampled from either a uniform (UHS) or data-driven (DHS) distribution.

Given a dataset $\mathcal{D}$ of measurements y, the objective is to minimize:

$$\underset{\phi}{\arg\min}\, \mathbb{E}_{\alpha \sim p(\alpha)} \sum_{y \in \mathcal{D}} \left[J(G_{H_\phi(\alpha)}(y), y) + \sum_{i=1}^{p} \alpha_i \mathcal{R}_i \left(G_{H_\phi(\alpha)}(y) \right) \right]. \quad (3)$$

In the hypothetical scenario of infinite hypernetwork capacity, the hypernetwork can capture a mapping of any input α to the optimal $\theta^* = H_{\phi^*}(\alpha)$ that minimizes Eq. (2) with the corresponding α. The training of the hypernetwork is not sample-limited, since one can draw as many hyperparameter samples as needed. Thus, overfitting for the hypernetwork is not a practical concern. However, in practice, we will have a limited capacity hypernetwork and its learned parameters will in general depend on the assumed distribution for α.

In general, the expression inside the braces of Eq. (3) can be manipulated such that the hyperparameter support is bounded to $\alpha \in [0,1]^p$. For example, for one and two regularization weights, we can use:

$$\mathcal{L}_{p=1}(y, \alpha) = (1 - \alpha_1) J(\hat{x}, y) + \alpha_1 \mathcal{R}_1(\hat{x}), \quad (4)$$

$$\mathcal{L}_{p=2}(y, \alpha) = \alpha_1 J(\hat{x}, y) + (1 - \alpha_1)\alpha_2\, \mathcal{R}_1(\hat{x}) + (1 - \alpha_1)(1 - \alpha_2)\, \mathcal{R}_2(\hat{x}), \quad (5)$$

where $\hat{x} = G_{H_\phi(\alpha)}(y)$ denotes the reconstruction.

3.2 Training

Uniform Hyperparameter Sampling (UHS): A straightforward strategy for training the hypernetwork involves sampling the regularization weights from a uniform distribution $p(\alpha) = U[0,1]^p$ and a measurement y from $\mathcal{D}$ for each forward pass during training. The gradients are then computed with respect to the loss evaluated at the sampled α via a backward pass. This corresponds to minimizing Eq. (3) with a uniform distribution for α.

However, the finite model capacity of the hypernetwork constrains the ability to achieve optimal loss for every hyperparameter value, particularly without resorting to training large hypernetworks. In addition, sampling hyperparameters from the entire support $[0, 1]^p$ might "waste" model capacity on regularization weight values which, when optimized, do not produce acceptable reconstructions. These two observations suggest that modifying the hyperparameter sampling distribution could lead to better performance by making better use of limited hypernetwork model capacity.

Data-Driven Hyperparameter Sampling (DHS): In the unsupervised scenario, we propose to use the DC loss induced by a setting of the regularization weights to assess whether the reconstruction will be useful or not. Intuitively, values of $\boldsymbol{\alpha}$ which lead to high DC loss $J(G_{H_\phi(\boldsymbol{\alpha})}(\boldsymbol{y}), \boldsymbol{y})$ will produce reconstructions that deviate too much from the underlying anatomy, and which therefore can be ignored during training.

To compute a dynamic DC threshold during training, we propose using the K samples with the lowest DC loss within a mini-batch of size $B > K$ to calculate the gradients. In effect, this dedicates model capacity for the subset of the hyperparameter landscape that can produce reconstructions that are most consistent with the data, while ignoring those that do not. The percentage of the landscape which is optimized is K/B.

4 Experiments

In all experiments, we restrict our attention to the case of $p = 2$ regularization functions, although we emphasize that our method works for any number of regularization loss terms. We choose layer-wise total ℓ_1-penalty on the weights θ of the main reconstruction network and the TV of the reconstruction image as two regularization loss terms.

Implementation. The reconstruction network consists of a residual U-Net architecture [28] with 64 hidden channels per encoder layer, yielding a total of $n = 592,002$ (non-trainable) parameters. The hypernetwork consists of fully-connected layers with leaky ReLU activations and BatchNorms between intermediate layers. Hypernetwork weights were initialized to approximate standard Kaiming initialization in the main network [7]. We experiment with three hypernetwork architectures, all fully-connected: "small" is 1-2-4-n, "medium" is 1-8-32-n, and "large" is 1-8-32-32-32-n, where numbers denote the width of the respective layer,

For all models and baselines, we set the mini-batch size to $B = 32$ and used ADAM optimizer. For DHS, we took the top 25% of samples within a mini-batch, i.e. $K = 8$, chosen using a grid-search, although we find that results are not very sensitive to this value. All training and testing experiments in this paper were performed on a machine equipped with an Intel Xeon Gold 6126 processor and an NVIDIA Titan Xp GPU. All models were implemented in Pytorch.

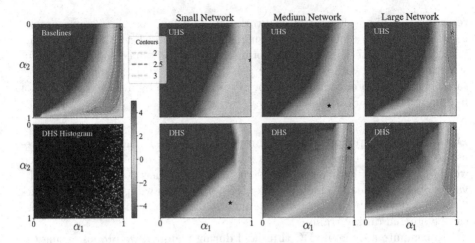

Fig. 2. RPSNR values over the hyperparameter support $[0,1]^2$ for different hypernetwork capacity and sampling methods. The x-axis and y-axis denote the value of the hyperparameters α_1 and α_2, respectively. Star denotes optimal hyperparameter values. Contours denote level sets of fixed value (see legend). (Left) The top image depicts the baseline landscape. The bottom image shows an example histogram of hyperparameter values used for gradient computation during one epoch of training with the DHS strategy. (Right) The top and bottom row show the UHS and DHS model landscapes, respectively, for three different hypernetwork capacities.

Data. We trained and evaluated networks on a dataset of T1-weighted axial brain images [11]. All images were intensity-normalized to the range $[0,1]$ and cropped and re-sampled to a pixel grid of size 256×256. Dataset splits were 2000, 500, and 1000 slices for training, validation, and testing. No subjects and scans were overlapping between the splits. Under-sampled measurements were obtained by retrospective down-sampling with 4-fold acceleration sub-sampling masks using a 2nd-order polynomial Poisson-disk variable-density sampling strategy [8,14,24].

Evaluation Metrics. Reconstructions were evaluated against ground-truth full-resolution images on peak signal-to-noise ratio (PSNR) and structural

Table 1. Training and inference time for proposed models. Inference time is the runtime of one forward pass with a single α and y input, averaged over the test set. Mean $\pm$ standard deviation. "$\sim$" denotes approximation.

Model	Sampling method	Training time (hr)	Inference time (sec)
Baselines	-	$\sim$648	0.208 ± 0.014
HyperRecon, Small	UHS	$\sim$6	0.241 ± 0.013
	DHS	$\sim$7	0.237 ± 0.016
HyperRecon, Medium	UHS	$\sim$12	0.256 ± 0.023
	DHS	$\sim$15	0.259 ± 0.021
HyperRecon, Large	UHS	$\sim$48	0.271 ± 0.013
	DHS	$\sim$55	0.275 ± 0.025

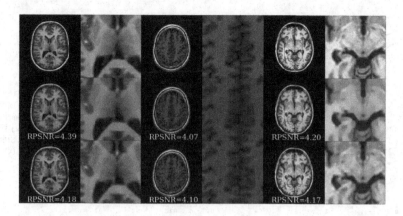

Fig. 3. Example slices, full-size and zoomed-in. First row are ground-truth images. Subsequent rows are reconstructions with similar RPSNR values (indicated) but computed with different regularization weights.

similarity index measure (SSIM). The *relative* value (RPSNR and RSSIM) was obtained by further subtracting the metric value for the zero-filled reconstruction, computed by applying the inverse Fourier transform directly to the zero-filled k-space data.

We also quantified the range of reconstructions that exceeded a RPSNR threshold. For this, we collected all above-threshold reconstructions, and computed the difference between the maximum and minimum value at every pixel. Finally, we summed these values over all pixels. This was treated as the range metric.

Baseline Models. For comparison, we trained 324 separate U-Net reconstruction networks for each fixed hyperparameter value, creating an 18×18 grid on the space $[0, 1]^2$. We refer to these models as benchmarks and emphasize that they demand significant computational resources, since each of these models need to be trained and saved separately (see Table 1 for run-times).

4.1 Hypernetwork Capacity and Hyperparameter Sampling

We evaluate the performance of the proposed models using RPSNR landscapes over the hyperparameter support $(\alpha_1, \alpha_2) \in [0, 1]^2$ in Fig. 2. We generated landscapes by sampling in $[0, 1]^2$ to create a grid of size 100×100. For each grid point, we computed the value by passing the corresponding hyperparameter values to the model along with each measurement $\boldsymbol{y}$ in the test set and taking the average RPSNR value.[2]

---

[2] For baselines, the 18×18 grid was linearly interpolated to 100×100 to match the hypernetwork landscapes.

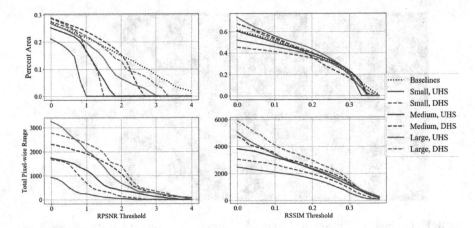

Fig. 4. (Top) Percent of hyperparameter support area vs. metric threshold. Values were calculated by computing the area in $[0,1]^2$ which exceeded the metric value. (Bottom) Total pixel-wise range vs. metric threshold. Values were calculated by collecting all reconstructions exceeding the metric value, computing the difference between the maximum and minimum pixel value for every pixel location across the set, and summing the result.

We observe that higher capacity hypernetworks approach the baseline models' performance, at the cost of increased computational resources and training time (see Table 1). We also observe significant improvement in performance using DHS as compared to UHS, given a fixed hypernetwork capacity. Black stars denote the optimal hyperparameter values; although this was found by maximum RPSNR value, rapid tuning using visual inspection can be done in the absence of full-resolution data.

We find that the performance improvement achieved by DHS is less for the large hypernetwork, validating the expectation that the sampling distribution plays a more important role when the hypernetwork capacity is restricted. In Fig. 4a, we quantify this by plotting the percent area that exceed a RPSNR threshold, for all models and baselines. Better-performing models have a larger area under the curve.

4.2   Range of Reconstructions

Figure 4b shows the reconstruction ranges of different models, with a larger area under the curve being desirable. We observe that higher capacity models and DHS yield a consistent increase in the range of reconstructions, compared to their lower capacity and UHS counterparts.

Figure 3 shows some example reconstructions computed by the DHS large model. For a ground truth, we selected two reconstructions within RPSNR range $[4, 4.5]$ and maximum ℓ_2 distance. In particular, we observe the difference in smoothness and sharp detail despite the overall quality of the reconstructions (as measured by RPSNR) being nearly identical.

5   Conclusion

We introduce HyperRecon, an CS-MRI reconstruction method that is agnostic to regularization-weight hyperparameters in the amortized optimization formulation. We propose a novel data-driven hyperparameter sampling method that boosts the performance of our proposed model, and show that it performs comparably to non-agnostic and computationally-prohibitive baselines. We furthermore highlight and quantify the range of reconstructions capable of being produced by our models. While our experiments focused on MRI reconstruction, this method can be applied broadly in order to render agnosticism towards any hyperparameter that may arise in many machine learning models.

Acknowledgements. This work was supported by NIH grants R01LM012719 (MS), R01AG053949 (MS), 1R01AG064027 (AD), the NSF NeuroNex grant 1707312 (MS), and the NSF CAREER 1748377 grant (MS).

References

1. Aggarwal, H.K., Mani, M.P., Jacob, M.: MoDL: Model-based deep learning architecture for inverse problems. IEEE Trans. Med. **38**(2), 394–405 (2019)
2. Balakrishnan, G., Zhao, A., Sabuncu, M.R., Guttag, J., Dalca, A.V.: Voxelmorph: a learning framework for deformable medical image registration. IEEE Trans. Med. **38**(8), 1788–1800 (2019)
3. Beck, A., Teboulle, M.: A fast iterative shrinkage-thresholding algorithm for linear inverse problems. SIAM J. Img. Sci. **2**(1), 183–202 (2009)
4. Boyd, S., Parikh, N., Chu, E., Peleato, B., Eckstein, J.: Distributed optimization and statistical learning via the alternating direction method of multipliers. Found. Trends Mach. Learn. **3**(1), 1–122 (2011)
5. Brock, A., Lim, T., Ritchie, J., Weston, N.: SMASH: one-shot model architecture search through hypernetworks. In: ICLR (2018)
6. Chambolle, A., Pock, T.: A first-order primal-dual algorithm for convex problems with applications to imaging. J. Math. Imag. Vis. **40**, 120–145 (2011)
7. Chang, O., Flokas, L., Lipson, H.: Principled weight initialization for hypernetworks. In: ICLR (2020)
8. Chauffert, N., Ciuciu, P., Weiss, P.: Variable density compressed sensing in MRI. theoretical vs heuristic sampling strategies. In: 2013 IEEE 10th ISBI, April 2013
9. Combettes, P.L., Pesquet, J.C.: Proximal splitting methods in signal processing (2009)
10. Cremer, C., Li, X., Duvenaud, D.: Inference suboptimality in variational autoencoders (2018)
11. Dalca, A.V., Guttag, J., Sabuncu, M.R.: Anatomical priors in convolutional networks for unsupervised biomedical segmentation. In: IEEE CVPR, June 2018
12. Daubechies, I., Defrise, M., Mol, C.D.: An iterative thresholding algorithm for linear inverse problems with a sparsity constraint. Pure Appl. Math. **57**, 1413 1457 (2003)
13. Figueiredo, M.A.T., Nowak, R.D.: An FM algorithm for wavelet-based image restoration. IEEE Trans. Image Process. **12**(8), 906–916 (2003)

14. Geethanath, S., et al.: Compressed sensing MRI: a review. Crit. Rev. Biomed. Eng. **41**(3), 183–204 (2013)

15. Gershman, S.J., Goodman, N.D.: Amortized inference in probabilistic reasoning. In: CogSci (2014)

16. Ha, D., Dai, A., Le, Q.V.: Hypernetworks (2016)

17. Hoopes, A., Hoffmann, M., Fischl, B., Guttag, J., Dalca, A.V.: Hypermorph: amortized hyperparameter learning for image registration. arXiv preprint arXiv:2101.01035 (2021)

18. Hu, Y., Jacob, M.: Higher degree total variation (HDTV) regularization for image recovery. IEEE Trans. Image Process. **21**(5), 2559–2571 (2012)

19. Kingma, D.P., Welling, M.: Auto-encoding variational bayes (2014)

20. Klocek, S., Maziarka, L., Wolczyk, M., Tabor, J., Nowak, J., Śmieja, M.: Hypernetwork functional image representation. Lecture Notes in Computer Science, pp. 496–510. (2019)

21. Krueger, D., Huang, C.W., Islam, R., Turner, R., Lacoste, A., Courville, A.: Bayesian hypernetworks (2018)

22. Lorraine, J., Duvenaud, D.: Stochastic hyperparameter optimization through hypernetworks (2018)

23. Luo, G.: A review of automatic selection methods for machine learning algorithms and hyper-parameter values. Netw. Model Anal. Health Inform. Bioinforma. **5**, 18 (2016). https://doi.org/10.1007/s13721-016-0125-6

24. Lustig, M., Donoho, D., Pauly, J.M.: Sparse MRI the application of compressed sensing for rapid MR imaging. Magn. Reson. Med. **58**(6), 1182–1195 (2007)

25. Marino, J., Yue, Y., Mandt, S.: Iterative amortized inference. arXiv preprint arXiv:1807.09356 (2018)

26. Pan, Z., Liang, Y., Zhang, J., Yi, X., Yu, Y., Zheng, Y.: Hyperst-net: hypernetworks for spatio-temporal forecasting (2018)

27. Ravishankar, S., Ye, J.C., Fessler, J.A.: Image reconstruction: from sparsity to data-adaptive methods and machine learning. Proc. IEEE **108**(1), 86–109 (2020)

28. Ronneberger, O., Fischer, P., Brox, T.: U-Net: convolutional networks for biomedical image segmentation. In: Navab, N., Hornegger, J., Wells, W.M., Frangi, A.F. (eds.) MICCAI 2015. LNCS, vol. 9351, pp. 234–241. Springer, Cham (2015). https://doi.org/10.1007/978-3-319-24574-4_28

29. Rudin, L.I., Osher, S., Fatemi, E.: Nonlinear total variation based noise removal algorithms. Phys. D Nonlin. Phenomena **60**(1–4), 259–268 (1992)

30. Shahriari, B., Swersky, K., Wang, Z., Adams, R.P., de Freitas, N.: Taking the human out of the loop: a review of Bayesian optimization. Proc. IEEE **104**(1), 148–175 (2016)

31. Shen, F., Yan, S., Zeng, G.: Meta networks for neural style transfer (2017)

32. Shu, R., Bui, H.H., Zhao, S., Kochenderfer, M.J., Ermon, S.: Amortized inference regularization (2018)

33. Ukai, K., Matsubara, T., Uehara, K.: Hypernetwork-based implicit posterior estimation and model averaging of CNN. In: Zhu, J., Takeuchi, I. (eds.) Proceedings of The 10th Asian Conference on Machine Learning. Proceedings of Machine Learning Research, vol. 95, pp. 176–191. PMLR, November 2018

34. Wang, A.Q., Dalca, A.V., Sabuncu, M.R.: Neural network-based reconstruction in compressed sensing MRI without fully-sampled training data. In: Deeba, F., Johnson, P., Würfl, T., Ye, J.C. (eds.) Machine Learning for Medical Image Reconstruction, pp. 27–37. Springer International Publishing, Cham (2020)

35. Wang, S., et al.: Accelerating magnetic resonance imaging via deep learning. In: 2016 IEEE 13th International Symposium on Biomedical Imaging (ISBI), pp. 514–517 (2016)
36. Yang, G., et al.: Dagan: deep de-aliasing generative adversarial networks for fast compressed sensing MRI reconstruction. IEEE Trans. Med. Imag. **37**(6), 1310–1321 (2018)
37. Yang, Y., Sun, J., Li, H., Xu, Z.: Deep admm-net for compressive sensing MRI. In: Lee, D., Sugiyama, M., Luxburg, U., Guyon, I., Garnett, R. (eds.) Advances in Neural Information Processing Systems. vol. 29. Curran Associates, Inc. Barcelona (2016)
38. Ye, N., Roosta-Khorasani, F., Cui, T.: Optimization methods for inverse problems. In: Wood, D., de Gier, J., Praeger, C., Tao, T. (eds.) 2017 MATRIX Annals. MATRIX Book Series, vol. 2, pp. 121–140. Springer, Cham (2019). https://doi.org/10.1007/978-3-030-04161-8_9
39. Yin, W., Osher, S., Goldfarb, D., Darbon, J.: Bregman iterative algorithms for l_1-minimization with applications to compressed sensing. SIAM J. Imag. Sci. **1**(1), 143–168 (2008)
40. Yu, T., Zhu, H.: Hyperparameter optimization. In: Hutter, F., Kotthoff, L., Vanschoren, J. (eds.) Automated Machine Learning. The Springer Series on Challenges in Machine Learning. Springer, Cham (2019). https://doi.org/10.1007/978-3-030-05318-5_1
41. Zhang, C., Ren, M., Urtasun, R.: Graph hypernetworks for neural architecture search (2019)

Efficient Image Registration Network for Non-Rigid Cardiac Motion Estimation

Jiazhen Pan[1(✉)], Daniel Rueckert[1,3], Thomas Küstner[2], and Kerstin Hammernik[1,3]

[1] Lab for AI in Medicine, Technical University of Munich, Munich, Germany
jiazhen.pan@tum.de
[2] Medical Image and Data Analysis (MIDAS.lab), University of Tübingen, Tübingen, Germany
[3] Department of Computing, Imperial College London, London, UK

Abstract. Cardiac motion estimation plays an essential role in motion-compensated cardiac Magnetic Resonance (MR) image reconstruction. In this work, we propose a robust and lightweight self-supervised deep learning registration framework, termed MRAFT, to estimate non-rigid cardiac motion. The proposed framework combines an efficient architecture with a novel degradation-restoration (DR) loss term, and an enhancement mask derived from a pre-trained segmentation network. This framework enables the prediction of both small and large cardiac motion more precisely, and allows us to handle through-plane motion in a 2D registration setting via the DR loss. The quantitative and qualitative experiments on a retrospective cohort of 42 in-house acquired 2D cardiac CINE MRIs indicate that the proposed method outperforms the competing approaches substantially, with more than 25% reduction in residual photometric error, and up to $100\times$ faster inference speed compared to conventional methods.

1 Introduction

In cardiac magnetic resonance imaging (CMR), CINE serves as the gold standard to assess cardiac morphology and function. Acquisition of cardiac motion-resolved CINE involves dealing with respiratory and cardiac motion. Respiratory motion is typically approached in CINE by breath-holds, whereas for the cardiac motion prospective ECG triggering or retrospective ECG gating are used. To ensure stable counting statistics, usually a few minutes of acquisition are required to handle and resolve the motion. Retrospective motion correction enables us to improve image quality and/or to reduce acquisition times. Various methods have been proposed that perform an implicit motion correction by leveraging spatio-temporal redundancy and enforcing sparseness/low-rankness

---

T. Küstner and K. Hammernik—Equal contribution.

Electronic supplementary material The online version of this chapter (https://doi.org/10.1007/978-3-030-88552-6_2) contains supplementary material, which is available to authorized users.

© Springer Nature Switzerland AG 2021
N. Haq et al. (Eds.): MLMIR 2021, LNCS 12964, pp. 14–24, 2021.
https://doi.org/10.1007/978-3-030-88552-6_2

along these dimensions [1–6]. Alternatively, motion correction can be explicitly embedded into the reconstruction process based on the idea of general matrix decomposition [12–14]. For these motion-compensated reconstructions, the estimation of a reliable motion model is essential and relies on image registration.

A number of registration approaches can be adopted to model the deformation operator that estimates the temporal motion during the reconstruction. Conventional methods like diffusion [15] or parametric B-Splines [16] have been proposed which have been integrated into various registration frameworks [17–19]. However, hyperparameter-tuning for these approaches [18,19], especially in the context of non-rigid cardiac motion, is a non-trivial task. Furthermore, these conventional registration methods are often associated with large computational costs and long execution times, making the potential clinical application impractical. In recent years, image registration and motion estimation have been recast as a learning-based approach. A variety of data-driven and deep learning-based motion correction methods have been proposed. U-Net [22] and FlowNet [23] exert a far-reaching impact in computer vision and inspired many image registration networks for CMR [25–27]. These CMR networks follow the backbone of FlowNet or U-Net, which means that they also inherit their drawbacks, e.g. the high number of trainable parameters (>30M) and the lack of accuracy because residual flow estimation is not performed. More recently, Motion Pyramid Network (MPN) [30] was proposed by Yu et al. Although MPN is more lightweight and outperforms FlowNet-based networks, its performance is limited by coarse-to-fine mechanism. While coarse-to-fine approaches are commonly used in motion estimation [17–19,28], they can have difficulties in recovering errors at the coarse level and tend to miss small fast-moving patterns.

In the context of CMR [7–11], large non-rigid motion across multiple temporal frames can occur and in the case of 2D imaging the existence of through-plane motion complicates the motion estimation process. Moreover, ground-truth cardiac motion is hard to collect or annotate, making supervised training infeasible. Using joint learning of two complementary networks [24] or a teacher-student and knowledge distillation mechanism [29] as in MPN [30] can alleviate the difficulty of unsupervised or self-supervised training. These two approaches build interactions between their sub-networks which can either guide the training of each other mutually or reinforce one by the other. However, one may argue that both are non-trivial to apply and train. For joint learning in [24], the segmentation and motion estimation networks are coupled, resulting in a complex architecture, where one malfunctioning network might mislead the training of the other. For the teacher-student mechanism in [30], a computational bottleneck arises because the teacher model needs to be frozen if the student network is in training. Thus, we investigate if we can keep the advantages from jointly trained networks or teacher-student networks while training only a single network.

In this work, we propose a novel cardiac motion estimation approach, named MRAFT, which is inspired by 4D All Pairs Correlation from [32] and the idea of self-supervision loss from [31]. Instead of using complex sub-network architectures, the proposed MRAFT addresses the aforementioned challenges within a single network. First, we apply a lightweight and efficient architecture without using the prevailing coarse-to-fine mechanism. Second, we propose a degradation-restoration (DR) loss as part of the regularization term to handle occlusion caused by large and through-plane motion. Third, we introduce an enhancement mask extracted from a pre-trained segmentation network [33] to emphasize the cardiac region. Finally, we train and evaluate the proposed MRAFT on in-house acquired 2D CINE data of 17 healthy subjects and 25 patients and compare the results to other state-of-the-art registration methods. The qualitative and quantitative experiments reveal that MRAFT outperforms both conventional and learning-based methods in terms of prediction accuracy and inference speed.

2   Method

In this section, we introduce MRAFT, a self-supervised framework for solving the non-rigid cardiac motion estimation problem.

2.1   Network Architecture

Given a pair of fixed I_f and moving I_m CMR images, the network $f(\cdot)$ with trainable parameters θ learns to estimate the two-dimensional deformation field $\mathbf{u} = [\mathbf{u}_x, \mathbf{u}_y]^\top$ between I_f and I_m,

$$\mathbf{u} = f(I_f, I_m; \theta) \tag{1}$$

RAFT [32] forms the backbone of the flow estimation network $f(\cdot)$ for the proposed MRAFT in Fig. 1. Following the principle of RAFT, single-channel images are first sent through a siamese feature encoder consisting of seven convolutional layers with a downsampling factor of 4. Then, a 4D pairs correlation block including a look-up operator, that covers the two-dimensional image and two-dimensional motion space, is applied. The image space here remains at high resolution without downsampling. Therefore, no small fast-moving objects are missed. Downsampling is only applied in the motion space, which enables the network to estimate and look up large and small motion. After that, the 4D correlation pairs and the extracted context features of the moving image are processed in Gated Recurrent Unit (GRU) blocks with shared parameters, which allow the network to refine the flow estimation and minimize the residual errors iteratively. Finally, the estimated motion field is bilinearly interpolated to the initial resolution. The proposed MRAFT contains 4M trainable parameters.

2.2   Self-supervised Loss Function

Photometric Loss. Following the work of [20,21], the photometric loss term is employed for robust motion estimation

$$\mathcal{L}_{\text{Ph,i}} = \sum_{\mathbf{p}} \rho\left(\Phi(\mathbf{p}) \cdot (I_c^{(i)}(\mathbf{p}) - I_f(\mathbf{p}))\right) \tag{2}$$

$$\text{with } I_c^{(i)} = I_m(\mathbf{p} + \mathbf{u}^{(i)}(\mathbf{p}))$$

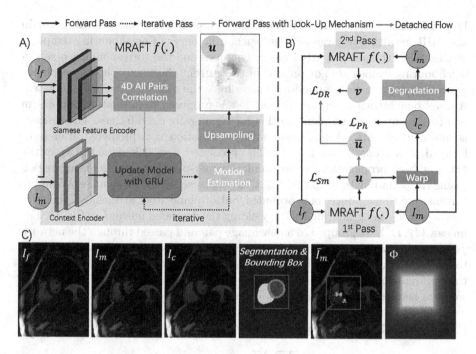

Fig. 1. A) Overview of MRAFT architecture. B) Overview of the estimation pipeline and loss function. C) Examples of (left to right) fixed image I_f, moving image I_m, motion-corrected image I_c, heart bounding box derived from cardiac segmentation of [33], degraded image $\bar{I}_m$ with Gaussian noise blocks within the bounding box, and enhancement mask Φ with exponential decay: yellow = 1, black = 0. (Color figure online)

where $\mathbf{p}$ is the 2D coordinates of image pixels, Φ denotes the cardiac mask introduced in Sect. 2.3, I_c refers to the motion-corrected image which is warped from I_m with the motion estimation $\mathbf{u}$ of the network f using bilinear interpolation, and i is the estimation, corrected image or losses at i-th iteration from GRU. $\rho(x) = (x^2 + \epsilon^2)^\omega$ is the Charbonnier penalty function [35] with $\epsilon = 1\text{e--}6$ and $\omega = 0.45$.

Smoothness Loss. If we would only consider the photometric loss, the generation of unrealistic flows and the well-known aperture problem can arise. Therefore, an edge-awareness smoothness regularization term is introduced to mitigate these problems along both x and y directions

$$\mathcal{L}_{\text{Sm,i}} = \sum_{d \in x,y} \sum_{\mathbf{P}} \left(|\nabla \mathbf{u}_d^{(i)}(\mathbf{p})| e^{-|\nabla_d I_m(\mathbf{p})|} \right) \tag{3}$$

A Laplace-alike penalty function $e^{-|\cdot|}$ is used to avoid over-smoothness at the corner or edge of the image, i.e. at areas of high image gradients.

Degradation-Restoration (DR) Loss. Through-plane motion can occur in 2D CMR, resulting in large morphological differences of neighbouring temporal frames. Since this motion arises in the long-axis and the corresponding pixels in neighbouring frames are not present in the current short-axis plane, the photometric assumption (corresponding images have the same grey value) is violated. A novel regularization term called DR loss is proposed to mitigate this problem and to simulate through-plane motion for temporally close frames. The concept is shown in Fig. 1B). A first-pass motion estimation $\mathbf{u}$ is predicted after feedforward pass according to Eq. (1). The predicted flow $\bar{\mathbf{u}}$ is detached from the gradient back-propagation. Then, random super-pixels within the heart region (using the bounding box from Sect. 2.3) are replaced by Gaussian noise. We apply this method to introduce some occluded/out-of-plane areas artificially. This process is named as degradation ("D"), yielding the degraded image $\bar{I}_m$ (Fig. 1). The images $\{I_f, \bar{I}_m\}$ are grouped as a new image pair and passed through the network $f(\cdot)$ a second time to predict $\mathbf{v}$. During this second pass, the network is forced to learn the restoration of these super-pixels which correspond to out-of-view or through-plane motion. But in contrast to the case of real through-plane motion, we have here the detached estimation $\bar{\mathbf{u}}$ serving as pseudo ground-truth, which can guide this challenging estimation process. This step is denoted as restoration ("R"). The DR loss can thus be formulated as

$$\mathcal{L}_{\text{DR}} = \sum_{d \in x, y} \sum_{\mathbf{P}} \rho \left(\bar{\mathbf{u}}_d(\mathbf{p}) - \mathbf{v}_d(\mathbf{p}) \right) \tag{4}$$

Finally, the total loss can be formulated as

$$\mathcal{L}_{total} = \sum_{i=1}^{N} \alpha^{N-i} \left(\mathcal{L}_{\text{Ph},i} + \beta \mathcal{L}_{\text{Sm},i} \right) + \gamma_t \mathcal{L}_{\text{DR}_N} \tag{5}$$

in which the photometric and smoothness losses are weighted exponentially by α over N GRU iterations. DR loss is only calculated on the last iteration to ensure that the network can deliver the most optimal estimation in the current training stage. Parameter γ_t is a stair-wise ascending weighting factor set to a small value at the beginning of training.

2.3   Enhancement Mask (EM)

To focus the registration towards the heart region, we introduce EM based on a pre-trained cardiac segmentation network [33]. A bounding box with a prescribed offset of 10 pixels around the segmented myocardium and left/right ventricles is placed. EM Φ with $\Phi(\mathbf{p}) = 1$ inside the bounding box and Laplacian decay of $\exp(-0.2 \cdot d)$ for distance d towards the periphery is employed to emphasize the heart region and to attenuate the influence of peripheral disturbances like respiratory motion blur and noise.

3   Experiments

Training was performed on 39 (15 healthy subjects and 24 patients) in-house acquired short-axis 2D CINE CMR, while testing was conducted on 3 (2 healthy subjects and 1 patient) left-out subjects. Data were acquired with 2D balanced steady-state free precession: TE = 1.06 ms, TR = 2.12 ms, image size = 176×132 with a stack of 12 slices along long-axis, resolution = $1.9 \times 1.9 \times$ mm^2, slice thickness=8 mm, 25 cardiac phases, 8 breath-holds of 15s duration. Apical slices without clear cardiac motion were excluded, resulting in 50000/180 image pairs for training/testing. Training image pairs were randomly augmented with photometric brightness and contrast perturbation. MRAFT was trained on an NVIDIA Quadro RTX 8000 with the batch size of 12, AdamW optimizer [34] and learning rate of 1e-4 with weight decay of 1e–5. The hyperparameters of MRAFT were $\alpha = 0.8$, $\beta = 10$, GRU iterations $N = 12$, and γ_t was initialized with 2 and doubled after every 5 epochs.

The proposed MRAFT was compared to NiftyReg [18], Elastix [19], Demons [17] and a learning-based method using an improved backbone based on [23] as conducted in [27] for an unsupervised loss with $\gamma = 1, \beta = 0.1$ (denoted as USFlow). An ablation study was conducted to investigate the contribution of EM and DR loss during the motion correction process.

4   Results

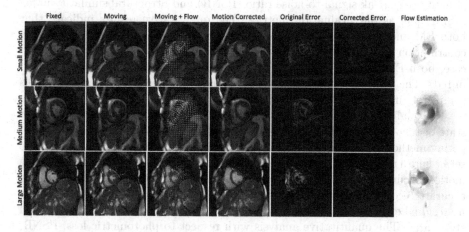

Fig. 2. Prediction results of MRAFT in terms of small (across 3 temporal frames), medium (across 5 temporal frames), and large motion (across 8 temporal frames) with instances of through-plane motion. The flow estimation is illustrated based on the color wheel proposed in [38]. (Color figure online)

Table 1. Quantitative comparison of MRAFT (ours) with state-of-the-art methods in terms of Photometric loss, PSNR, SSIM and averaged inference time.

Methods	Photo-Loss	PSNR	SSIM	Time (s)
Demons [17]	5.842 (2.390)	30.367 (3.412)	0.949 (0.031)	2.074
Elastix [19]	6.092 (2.879)	30.209 (4.047)	0.948 (0.033)	6.849
NiftyReg [18]	7.909 (3.378)	27.902 (3.858)	0.928 (0.042)	2.500
USFlow [23, 27]	6.735 (2.867)	29.128 (3.771)	0.934 (0.047)	**0.021**
MRAFT (ours)	**4.332** (1.564)	**33.298** (2.963)	**0.962** (0.026)	0.028

Figure 2 shows the estimation results of MRAFT in terms of small, medium and large deformations. In the first two cases, MRAFT can predict motion estimations precisely and results in minimal residual warping errors. In the last case, a systolic and end-diastolic frame (large temporal distance) are selected, where large deformations and through-plane motion occur. MRAFT is not obstructed by these challenges and yields a reasonable prediction. The flow estimation figures indicate that the cardiac region is well recognized and no erroneous estimations are made in the static background area in all three examples.

The qualitative and quantitative evaluations of the ablation study are illustrated in Supplementary Fig. 1 and Supplementary Table 1. Due to the lack of a gold standard ground-truth for the deformation field, quantitative results can only be interpreted in relation to each other. Here, we choose photometric loss (Photo-Loss), peak signal-to-noise ratio (PSNR) and Structural similarity index (SSIM) [36] as our evaluation metrics. The quantitative results indicate that both EM and DR loss improve the motion estimation accuracy, although the contribution of EM is limited. However, for the illustrated difficult large motion case, both EM and DR can contribute to control estimation artifacts (marked in red). The residual estimation error is primarily reduced by DR, and vanishes completely if EM is additionally considered.

The qualitative and quantitative superior performance of MRAFT to other state-of-the-art methods is demonstrated in Fig. 3 and Table 1. Since the competing methods are all capable of estimating small motions to some extent, we select here a challenging example in which large motion and severe through-plane motion occur. MRAFT substantially outperforms the other methods with the accurate recovery of moving structures like the papillary muscles, with almost no residual error left in the heart and no erroneous estimation in the peripheral static area. The quantitative analysis with respect to photometric loss, PSNR, SSIM and averaged inference time is shown in Table 1. Learning-based methods have a considerably shorter run-time because of their inherently trained parameters. MRAFT shows a more consistent performance with higher accuracy and lower standard deviations.

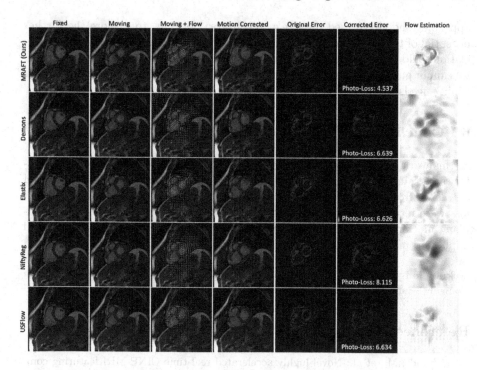

Fig. 3. Estimation of a challenging example with large and through-plane motion using MRAFT, Demons [17], Elastix [19], NiftyReg [18] and USFlow [23,27].

5   Discussion

Accurate and fast assessment of cardiac motion is essential for the analysis of ventricular function, identification of cardiovascular diseases or for the usage within intra- or inter-modality motion-compensated reconstructions. The proposed MRAFT provides a more accurate motion estimation than previously proposed methods and can precisely register cardiac phases even for large or through-plane motions. The lightweight 2D architecture of MRAFT targets image registration for the 2D imaging scenario, and achieves short inference times.

However, we also acknowledge some limitations of this work. Currently, we only focus on the application in 2D CINE. We will extend MRAFT for 3D imaging data which will also allow us to evaluate the estimation performance of through-plane-motion in the context of 2D cardiac CINE. Since acquisition of ground-truth cardiac motion is not possible, we will evaluate in future work the obtained cardiac flows in relation to cardiac functional assessment and clinically indicated functional motion patterns [37]. Furthermore, the used data were acquired and reconstructed in high quality with no motion blur and noise in peripheries. This makes the contribution of EM less forceful, which can only be sensed in visual inspection with large motion. In our future work, we will apply peripherally noised data (e.g. respiratory motion) to explore the further potential of the proposed EM. Finally, although the current MRAFT parameterization yields already superior results to its conventional comparative methods, we cannot guarantee that this setting is optimized, and a future hyper-parameter tuning needs to be conducted.

6   Conclusion

In this work, we proposed a lightweight self-supervised network with a straightforward training strategy to estimate non-rigid cardiac motion. Furthermore, EM extracted from a segmentation network to localize the cardiac region, and DR loss were introduced to guide the training and to deal with large and throughplane motion. We have confidence that this approach can be generalized and applied to more versatile registration tasks.

Acknowledgements. This work was supported in part by the European Research Council (Grant Agreement no. 884622).

References

1. Schmidt, M., et al.: Novel highly accelerated real-time CINE-MRI featuring compressed sensing with k-t regularization in comparison to TSENSE segmented and real-time Cine imaging. J. Cardiovasc. Magn. Reson. **15**, P36 (2013)
2. Hansen, M.S., Sorensen, T.S., Arai, A.E., Kellman, P.: Retrospective reconstruction of high temporal resolution cine images from real-time MRI using iterative motion correction. Magn. Reson. Med. **68**(3), 741–750 (2012)
3. Feng, L., et al.: 5D whole-heart sparse MRI. Magn. Reson. Med. **79**(2), 826–838 (2018)
4. Coppo, S., et al.: Free-running 4D whole-heart self-navigated golden angle MRI: initial results. Magn. Reson. Med. **74**(5), 1306–16 (2015)
5. Usman M., Ruijsink B., Nazir, et al. Free breathing whole-heart 3D CINE MRI with self-gated Cartesian trajectory. Magn Reson Imaging, 38:129–137, 2017
6. Küstner, T., Bustin, A., et al.: Fully self-gated free-running 3D Cartesian cardiac CINE with isotropic whole-heart coverage in less than 2 min. NMR Biomed. **34**(1), e4409 (2021)
7. Liu, F., Li, D., Jin, X., Qiu, W., Xia, Q., Sun, B.: Dynamic cardiac MRI reconstruction using motion aligned locally low rank tensor (MALLRT). Magn. Reson. Imaging **66**, 104–115 (2020)
8. Mohsin, Y.Q., Poddar, S., Jacob, M.: Free-breathing and ungated cardiac MRI using iterative SToRM (i-SToRM). IEEE Trans. Med. Imaging **38**(10), 2303–2313 (2019)
9. Lingala, S.G., Hu, Y., DiBella, E., Jacob, M.: Accelerated dynamic MRI exploiting sparsity and low-rank structure: k-t SLR. IEEE Trans. Med. Imaging **30**(5), 1042–1054 (2011)
10. Mohsin, Y.Q., Lingala, S.G., DiBella, E., Jacob, M.: Accelerated dynamic MRI using patch regularization for implicit motion compensation. Magn. Reson. Med. **77**(3), 1238–1248 (2017)

11. Küstner, T., Bustin, A., Jaubert, O., Hajhosseiny, R., Masci, P.G., Neji, R., Botnar, R., Prieto, C.: Isotropic 3D Cartesian single breath-hold CINE MRI with multi-bin patch-based low-rank reconstruction. Magn. Reson. Med. **84**(4), 2018–2033 (2020)
12. Batchelor, P.G., Atkinson, D., Irarrazaval, P., Hill, D.L.G., Hajnal J., Larkman. D.: Matrix description of general motion correction applied to multishot images. Magn. Reson. Med. **54**(5), 1273–1280 (2005)
13. Odille, F., Vuissoz, P.A., Marie, P.Y., et al.: Generalized reconstruction by inversion of coupled systems (GRICS) applied to free-breathing MRI. Magn. Reson. Med. **60**(1), 146–157 (2008)
14. Bustin, A., et al.: 3D whole-heart isotropic sub-millimeter resolution coronary magnetic resonance angiography with non-rigid motion-compensated PROST. J. Cardiovasc. Magn. Reson. **22**, 24 (2020)
15. Thirion, J.P.: Image matching as a diffusion process: an analogy with Maxwell's demons. Med. Image Anal. **2**(3), 243–260 (1998)
16. Rueckert, D., Sonoda, L.I., Hayes, C., et al.: Nonrigid registration using free-form deformations: application to breast MR images. IEEE Trans. Med. Imaging **18**(8), 712–721 (1999)
17. Vercauteren, T., Pennec, X., Perchant, A., Ayache, N.: Diffeomorphic demons: efficient non-parametric image registration. Neuroimage **45**(1), 61–72 (2009)
18. Modat, M., Ridgway, G.R., Taylor, Z.A., et al.: Fast free-form deformation using graphics processing units. Comput. Meth. Prog. Bio. **98**(3), 278–284 (2010)
19. Klein, S., Staring, M., Murphy, K., Viergever, M.A., Pluim, J.P.: Elastix: a toolbox for intensity-based medical image registration. IEEE Trans. Med. Imaging **29**(1), 196–205 (2010)
20. Horn, B.K., Schunck, B.G.: Determining optical flow. Artif. Intell. **17**(1), 185–203 (1981)
21. Brox, T., Bruhn, A., Papenberg, N., Weickert, J.: High accuracy optical flow estimation based on a theory for warping. In: European Conference on Computer Vision (ECCV), pp. 25–36 (2004)
22. Ronneberger, O., Fischer, P., Brox, T.: U-Net: convolutional Networks for Biomedical Image Segmentation. In: Navab, N., Hornegger, J., Wells, W.M., Frangi, A.F. (eds.) MICCAI 2015. LNCS, vol. 9351, pp. 234–241. Springer, Cham (2015). https://doi.org/10.1007/978-3-319-24574-4_28
23. Dosovitskiy, A., Fischer, P., Ilg, E., et al.: Flownet: learning optical flow with convolutional networks. In: IEEE International Conference on Computer Vision (ICCV), pp. 2758–2766 (2015)
24. Qin, C., et al.: Joint learning of motion estimation and segmentation for cardiac MR image sequences. In: International Conference on Medical Image Computing and Computer-Assisted Intervention (MICCAI), Springer, pp. 472–480 (2018)
25. Morales, M., Izquierdo-Garcia, D., Aganj, I., Kalpathy-Cramer, J., Rosen, B., Catana, C.: Implementation and validation of a three-dimensional cardiac motion estimation network. Radiol. Artif. Intell. **1**(4):e180080 (2019)
26. Zheng, Q., Delingette, H., Ayache, N.: Explainable cardiac pathology classification on cine MRI with motion characterization by semi-supervised learning of apparent flow. Med. Image Anal. **56**, 80–95 (2019)
27. Qi, H., et al.: Non-rigid respiratory motion estimation of whole-heart coronary MR images using unsupervised deep learning. IEEE Trans. Med. Imaging **41**(1), 444–454 (2021)
28. Sun, D., Yang, X., Liu, M., Kautz J. PWC-Net: CNNs for optical flow using pyramid, warping, and cost volume. In: IEEE Conference on Computer Vision and Pattern Recognition (CVPR), pp. 8934–8943 (2018)

29. Liu, P., King, I., Lyu, M.R., Xu, J.: DDflow: learning optical flow with unlabeled data distillation. In: The AAAI Conference on Artificial Intelligence, vol. 33, no. 1 (2019)

30. Yu, H., Chen, X., Shi, H., Chen, T., Huang, T.S., Sun, S.: Motion pyramid networks for accurate and efficient cardiac motion estimation. In: Martel, A.L., et al. (eds.) MICCAI 2020. LNCS, vol. 12266, pp. 436–446. Springer, Cham (2020). https://doi.org/10.1007/978-3-030-59725-2_42

31. Jonschkowski, R., Stone, A., Barron, J.T., Gordon, A., Konolige, K., Angelova, A.: What matters in unsupervised optical flow. arXiv preprint arXiv:2006.04902 (2020)

32. Teed, Z., Deng, J.: RAFT: recurrent all-pairs field transforms for optical flow. In: European Conference on Computer Vision (ECCV), pp. 402–419 (2020)

33. Bai, W., et al.: Automated cardiovascular magnetic resonance image analysis with fully convolutional networks. J. Cardiovasc. Magn. Reson. 20, 65 (2018)

34. Loshchilov, I., Hutter, F.: Decoupled weight decay regularization. arXiv preprint arXiv:1711.05101 (2017)

35. Sun, D., Roth, S., Black, M.J.: A quantitative analysis of current practices in optical flow estimation and the principles behind them. Int. J. Comput. Vis. 106(2), 115–137 (2014)

36. Zhou, W., Bovik, A.C., Sheikh, H.R., et al.: Image quality assessment: from error visibility to structural similarity. IEEE Trans. Image Process. 13(4), 600–612 (2004)

37. Lopez-Perez, A., Sebastian, R., Ferrero, J.M.: Three-dimensional cardiac computational modelling: methods, features and applications. Biomed. Eng. 14(1), 35 (2015)

38. Baker, S., Scharstein, D., Lewis, J., Roth, S., Black, M.J., Szeliski, R.: A database and evaluation methodology for optical flow. Int. J. Comput. Vis. 92(1), 1–31 (2011)

Evaluation of the Robustness of Learned MR Image Reconstruction to Systematic Deviations Between Training and Test Data for the Models from the fastMRI Challenge

Patricia M. Johnson[1]([✉]), Geunu Jeong[2], Kerstin Hammernik[3,14],
Jo Schlemper[4], Chen Qin[3,15], Jinming Duan[3,16], Daniel Rueckert[3,14],
Jingu Lee[2], Nicola Pezzotti[5], Elwin De Weerdt[10], Sahar Yousefi[6],
Mohamed S. Elmahdy[6], Jeroen Hendrikus Franciscus Van Gemert[10],
Christophe Schülke[11], Mariya Doneva[11], Tim Nielsen[11], Sergey Kastryulin[12],
Boudewijn P. F. Lelieveldt[6], Matthias J. P. Van Osch[6], Marius Staring[6],
Eric Z. Chen[7], Puyang Wang[8], Xiao Chen[7], Terrence Chen[7], Vishal M. Patel[8],
Shanhui Sun[7], Hyungseob Shin[13], Yohan Jun[13], Taejoon Eo[13], Sewon Kim[13],
Taeseong Kim[13], Dosik Hwang[13], Patrick Putzky[17], Dimitrios Karkalousos[18],
Jonas Teuwen[19], Nikita Miriakov[19], Bart Bakker[5], Matthan Caan[18],
Max Welling[17], Matthew J. Muckley[9], and Florian Knoll[1]

[1] Department of Radiology, NYU Langone Health, New York, NY, USA
patricia.johnson3@nyulangone.org
[2] AIRS Medical, Seoul, Korea
[3] Department of Computing, Imperial College London, London, UK
[4] Hyperfine Research Inc., Guilford, CT, USA
[5] Philips Research, Eindhoven, The Netherlands
[6] Department of Radiology, Leiden University Medical Center,
Leiden, The Netherlands
[7] United Imaging Intelligence, Cambridge, USA
[8] Department of Electrical and Computer Engineering, Johns Hopkins University,
Baltimore, MD, USA
[9] Facebook AI Research, New York, NY, USA
[10] Philips Healthcare, Best, The Netherlands
[11] Philips Research, 22335 Hamburg, Germany
[12] Philips Research, 121205 Moscow, Russia
[13] Department of Electrical and Electronic Engineering, Yonsei University, Seoul,
South Korea
[14] AI in Healthcare and Medicine, Klinikum Rechts der Isar, Technical University
of Munich, Munich, Germany
[15] Institute for Digital Communications, School of Engineering,
University of Edinburgh, Edinburgh, UK
[16] School of Computer Science, University of Birmingham, Birmingham, UK
[17] Amsterdam Machine Learning Lab, University of Amsterdam,
Amsterdam, The Netherlands
[18] Department of Biomedical Engineering and Physics,
Amsterdam UMC, University of Amsterdam, Amsterdam, The Netherlands
[19] Radboud University Medical Center, Netherlands Cancer Institute,
Amsterdam, The Netherlands

© Springer Nature Switzerland AG 2021
N. Haq et al. (Eds.): MLMIR 2021, LNCS 12964, pp. 25–34, 2021.
https://doi.org/10.1007/978-3-030-88552-6_3

Abstract. The 2019 fastMRI challenge was an open challenge designed to advance research in the field of machine learning for MR image reconstruction. The goal for the participants was to reconstruct undersampled MRI k-space data. The original challenge left an open question as to how well the reconstruction methods will perform in the setting where there is a systematic difference between training and test data. In this work we tested the generalization performance of the submissions with respect to various perturbations, and despite differences in model architecture and training, all of the methods perform very similarly.

1   Introduction

The goal of the 2019 fastMRI challenge [9] was to evaluate the performance of current state of the art machine learning methods for MR image reconstruction [2–4,7,8,15,19–21,25] on a large-scale standardized dataset [10,23]. The goal for the participants was to reconstruct images from undersampled MRI k-space data, and the challenge consisted of three tracks: For 2 tracks, we provided the original multi-receive channel data from MR scanners, and the tracks differed in the undersampling rate (R = 4 and R = 8). In the third track, we provided simulated single-channel data, which reduced the computational burden and reduced the learning curve of working with MR data. We received 33 total submissions, and during the course of the challenge, we identified the top 4 submissions per track in terms of structural similarity [18] to the fully sampled ground truth as finalists. These results of these top 4 finalists were then evaluated in a second stage of the challenge by clinical radiologists, which ultimately determined the winners of the challenge. An overview of example results from the finalists of each track is given in Fig. 1.

The winners presented their methods during the 2019 NeurIPS conference, and a detailed description of the structure of the challenge, the evaluation criteria and the results, are presented in [9]. The challenge prompted several follow up questions that were out of scope of the original evaluation. In particular, the challenge design did not include any type of domain shift between the training data and the challenge test data. Therefore, the generalization performance of the submissions with respect to perturbations was not tested. The presentations at the 2019 NeurIPS conference also raised the interesting point that in some test examples, despite providing visually and quantitatively impressive results, the reconstructions removed important image features.

In this work we systematically investigate the robustness of the approaches of the challenge finalists with respect to representative domain shifts in the data, which could occur in real-world clinical use. To this extent, we added certain perturbations to the challenge test set, and the finalists re-ran the models from their submissions without re-training. We also provide a more detailed follow-up analysis of the examples where pathology was missed in the original submissions.

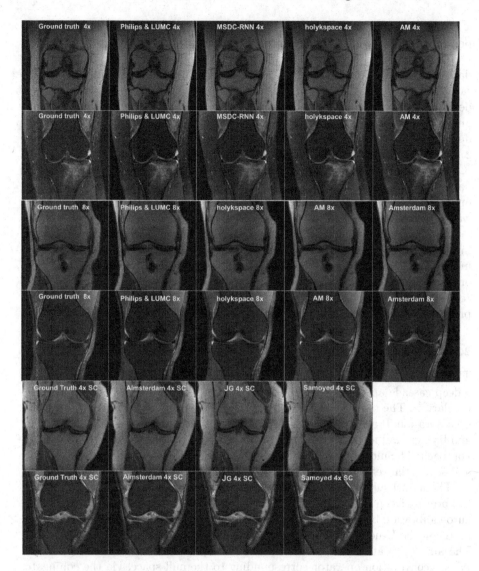

Fig. 1. Image results for the 2019 fastMRI knee challenge. Example results for the multicoil track R = 4, are shown in the top two rows, results for multicoil track R = 8 are shown in the middle two rows, and single coil results are shown in the bottom rows.

2 Methods

2.1 Image Perturbations

In the first set of experiments, we evaluate the response of the different methods to small structural changes in the images by in-painting objects to a proton density weighted image. We added squares with varying intensities (Fig. 2) and a resolution grid (Fig. 3), and then regenerate a simulated k-space from the perturbed image, which was reconstructed with each model.

To evaluate the effect of a mismatched SNR between the training and test data on network performance, we added noise to the input k-space of a fat-saturated data set. The noise level was estimated by calculating the standard deviation (σ) of voxel intensities from a slice with no anatomy. Two different amounts of noise were then added to the k-space. Gaussian noise with a standard deviation of 0.5σ and σ were added to the model input, simulating an SNR of 2/3 and 1/2 of the original SNR of the image.

The next experiment evaluates the robustness of each method when the input data has a different number of coils. We performed coil compression on the original 15 channel data, simulating 10 and 5 channel data. Coil compression was performed using the scipy SVD algorithm.

The final experiments explored two cases in which pathology was removed in the challenge reconstructions. For each case, the data were retrospectively under-sampled with two realizations of random under-sampling, including the original sampling pattern used in the challenge. The sampling patterns were consistent with $R = 4$ or $R = 8$ random under sampling commonly used in compressed sensing. In addition, we sampled 16 lines at the center of k-space.

2.2   Description of 2019 fastMRI Approaches

The network from Philips & LUMC, referred to as Adaptive-CS-Network [12], is a deep cascade approach that builds on the ISTA-Net model using a multiscale regularizer. The model consists of 25 unrolled iterations, with different design in each iteration. It also includes the MR physics priors, such as the phase behaviour and background identification, which are provided to the model with a "nudge" approach. The model is trained using a Multiscale-SSIM combined with L1 loss, and sequential refinement on different data populations.

The model submitted by AIRS medical (labelled as AM and JG) is an Auto-Calibrating Deep Learning Network. It consists of a neural network block and an auto-calibration block, which were iteratively applied. The neural network block, based on the U-net, was trained in combined complex image space with l1 loss. The auto-calibration block enforced the null space constraint $Nx = 0$, where N is a convolution operator corresponding to the null space, via the conjugate gradient method [16]. After the multiple cascade of the blocks, a refinement U-net processed the complex data and generated magnitude images.

The model originally referred to as MSDC-RNN is a Pyramid Convolutional RNN (PC-RNN) model [17], which includes three convolutional RNN modules to iteratively reconstruct images at different scales. The spatial sizes of feature maps in the three convolutional RNN modules are downsampled by $4\times$, $2\times$, $1\times$, respectively. Each convolutional RNN module has five iterations. The reconstructed images in coarse to fine scales are combined by a final CNN module. The model takes the multiple coils as multi-channel inputs and was trained with the NMSE loss [23] and the SSIM loss [24] on the coil combined images for 60 epochs.

Σ-Net [5] by holykspace (Imperial College London) ensembles multiple learned unrolled reconstruction networks. First, sensitivity networks involving explicit coil sensitivity maps were trained for a gradient descent, proximal gradient, and variable splitting scheme, followed by style transfer for further fine-tuning to the reference. Second, parallel coil networks were deployed to learn the coil combination implicitly. All networks, with a Down-Up Network as backbone [22], were unrolled for 10 steps. Training was conducted with a combined L1+SSIM loss, followed by individual fine-tuning for contrasts and acceleration factors. Additional networks trained with a GAN loss and a self-supervised approach complete the final ensemble of Σ-Net.

The Amsterdam submission is the i-RIM model [14] an invertible variant of the RIM [13] for reconstructing accelerated MR-images [11]. The 480-layers model consists of 12 down-sampling blocks. Except the zero-filled reconstruction, a 1-hot vector was also given as input for encoding field-strength and fat-suppression meta-data. For singlecoil data we chose 64 feature layers and for multicoil 96. For multicoil data, k-space measurements and individual coil images were stacked, without sensitivity modeling in this context. We cropped the images to 368×368 pixels, and for smaller sizes we applied zero-padding. Finally, we used the Adam optimizer with learning-rate 10-4, and the SSIM as loss function.

The Samoyed model utilizes consecutive CNN blocks in the image domain for de-aliasing [1,6], with interleaved data consistency layers that adopt trainable regularization parameters [3,15]. Each CNN block comprises 5 dilated convolutional layers with 64 feature maps followed by Leaky Rectified Linear Units. Every feature map of the 4th convolutional layer in each block is concatenated to the feature map of the 2nd convolutional layer in the next block (i.e., dense-connection) to prevent information wash-out. The L1 loss and the SSIM loss were applied only to the foreground area, so that the learning could be focused on the anatomical area rather than the background area. The model was separately trained on each acquisition protocol due to SNR mismatch.

All the finalists methods make use of some sort of data-consistency, demonstrating the importance of leveraging the data early in the reconstruction chain compared to techniques that rely solely on the reconstructed images.

3   Results

The performance of the submissions with respect to small structural changes are shown in Figs. 2 and 3. The first perturbation, which consists of 6 in-painted squares of varying intensities, appears blurred in all reconstructed images. This is consistent between tracks and for all submissions. In the multi-coil $R = 4$ reconstructions (Fig. 2, top row) the highest and lowest signal intensity squares remain distinguishable. We observe blurring and ghosting of the in-painted resolution grids in the $R = 4$ reconstructions shown in Fig. 3. This effect is more significant for the lower grid with vertical lines. In the $R = 8$ reconstructions, the resolution grids are almost completely removed.

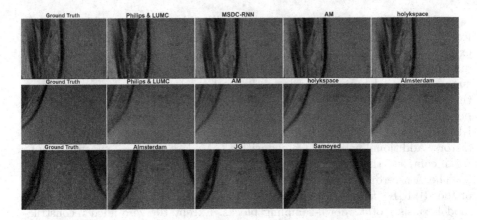

Fig. 2. Image results for contrast experiments. The perturbation is a set of in-painted squares with varying intensity. The R = 4, R = 8 and single coil results are shown in the top, middle and bottom rows respectively.

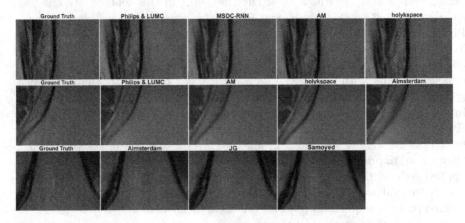

Fig. 3. Image results for resolution experiments. The perturbation is an in-painted resolution grid. The R = 4, R = 8 and single coil results are shown in the top, middle and bottom rows respectively

The performance of the submissions with respect to increased noise is shown in Fig. 4. A systematic mismatch in SNR between training and test data results in reconstructed images that appear over-smoothed. The Philips & LUMC reconstructions have lower SSIM but appear less smooth than reconstructions from other methods.

Most of the methods appear to be robust to a mismatch in the number of coils between the training and test data. The image quality is very similar for the reconstructions of 5, 10 and 15 channel data. The exception is the Amsterdam model, for which sensitivity maps were not included during training, but rather each coil image was treated as a separate channel. Results of the coil compression experiments for R = 8 are shown in Fig. 5.

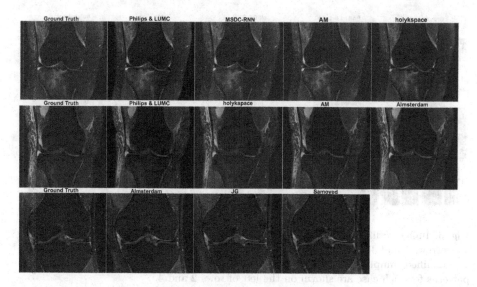

Fig. 4. Image results for noise experiments. Gaussian noise was added to the input k-space. The $R = 4$, $R = 8$ and single coil results are shown in the top, middle and bottom rows respectively

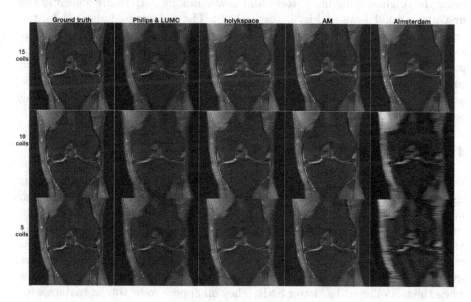

Fig. 5. Image results for $R = 8$ coil compression experiments. The network input was 5, 10 and 15 coils

Two cases from the original challenge where readers identified missing or less visible pathology in the reconstructed images were under-sampled with a different random sampling pattern with equivalent acceleration. The first case was a

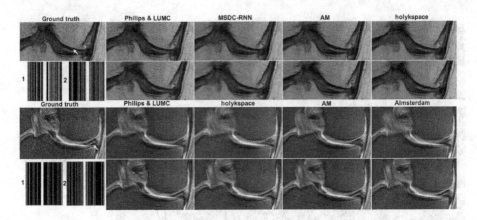

Fig. 6. Image results for two different sampling patterns. The original sampling patterns (rows 1 and 3) resulted in removed pathology. The pathology is more visible with the modified sampling pattern (rows 2 and 4). The original (1) and new (2) sampling patterns for each case are shown on the left of rows 2 and 4.

proton density weighted image with an acceleration of $R = 4$, the reconstructions using the original sampling pattern and new sampling pattern are shown in the first and second rows of Fig. 6, respectively. The pathology, indicated by the arrow in the ground truth image is more visible on the new reconstructions. The second case is a fat saturated image with acceleration $R = 8$. The reconstructions using the original and new sampling patterns are shown in the third and fourth row of Fig. 6 respectively. In this example the meniscal tear (indicated by the arrow in the ground truth image) is much more clear with the second sampling pattern than the original.

4   Discussion and Conclusion

In this work we evaluate the robustness of deep learning reconstruction methods submitted to the 2019 fastMRI challenge. All of these methods achieved high image quality but their robustness to possible domain shifts between training and test data remained an open question. In real world clinical use, the images may have unique features not seen in the training data, and they may vary in terms of SNR and coil configuration. Our results show that all of the methods remove small structures not seen in the training data and generate over smoothed images when the model input has lower SNR. They all appear to be robust to data with different coil configurations. We performed a follow-up analysis of the examples where pathology was missed in the original challenge reconstructions. Using a new realization of a random undersampling pattern with matched acceleration factors, the pathology was preserved. This suggests that the choice of sampling pattern can make a substantial difference in the clinical value of the image.

All DL reconstruction methods discussed in this work provide impressive results in the absence of a domain shift between training and test data. Our results show that all methods perform remarkably similarly in the presence of several perturbations despite differences in network architecture and training as well as showing the importance of the right sampling pattern for the reconstruction quality.

References

1. Accelerating cartesian MRI by domain-transform manifold learning in phase-encoding direction. Med. Image Anal. **63**, 101689 (2020)
2. Aggarwal, H.K., Mani, M.P., Jacob, M.: MoDL: model-based deep learning architecture for inverse problems. IEEE Trans. Med. Imaging **38**(2), 394–405 (2018)
3. Eo, T., Jun, Y., Kim, T., Jang, J., Lee, H.J., Hwang, D.: KIKI-net: cross-domain convolutional neural networks for reconstructing undersampled magnetic resonance images. Magn. Reson. Med. **80**(5), 2188–2201 (2018)
4. Hammernik, K., et al.: Learning a variational network for reconstruction of accelerated MRI data. Magn. Reson. Med. **79**(6), 3055–3071 (2018)
5. Hammernik, K., Schlemper, J., Qin, C., Duan, J., Summers, R.M., Rueckert, D.: Σ-Net: ensembled iterative deep neural networks for accelerated parallel MR image reconstruction. In: Proceedings of the International Society of Magnetic Resonance in Medicine (ISMRM), p. 0987 (2020)
6. Jun, Y., Eo, T., Shin, H., Kim, T., Lee, H.J., Hwang, D.: Parallel imaging in time-of-flight magnetic resonance angiography using deep multistream convolutional neural networks. Magn. Reson. Med. **81**(6), 3840–3853 (2019)
7. Knoll, F., Hammernik, K., Kobler, E., Pock, T., Recht, M.P., Sodickson, D.K.: Assessment of the generalization of learned image reconstruction and the potential for transfer learning. Magn. Reson. Med. **81**(1), 116–128 (2019). https://doi.org/10.1002/mrm.27355
8. Knoll, F., et al.: Deep-learning methods for parallel magnetic resonance imaging reconstruction: a survey of the current approaches, trends, and issues. IEEE Sig. Process. Mag. **37**(1), 128–140 (2020). https://doi.org/10.1109/MSP.2019.2950640
9. Knoll, F., et al.: Advancing machine learning for MR image reconstruction with an open competition: overview of the 2019 fastMRI challenge. Magn. Reson. Med. (2020). https://doi.org/10.1002/mrm.28338
10. Knoll, F., et al.: fastMRI: a publicly available raw k-space and DICOM dataset of knee images for accelerated MR image reconstruction using machine learning. Radiol. Artif. Intell. **2**(1), e190007 (2020)
11. Lønning, K., Putzky, P., Sonke, J.J., Reneman, L., Caan, M.W., Welling, M.: Recurrent inference machines for reconstructing heterogeneous MRI data. Med. Image Anal. **53**, 64–78 (2019)
12. Pezzotti, N., et al.: An adaptive intelligence algorithm for undersampled knee MRI reconstruction. IEEE Access **8**, 204825–204838 (2020). https://doi.org/10.1109/ACCESS.2020.3034287
13. Putzky, P., Welling, M.: Recurrent inference machines for solving inverse problems (2017)
14. Putzky, P., Welling, M.: Invert to learn to invert. In: Wallach, H., Larochelle, H., Beygelzimer, A., d'Alché-Buc, F., Fox, E., Garnett, R. (eds.) Advances in Neural Information Processing Systems, vol. 32. Curran Associates, Inc. (2019). https://proceedings.neurips.cc/paper/2019/file/ac1dd209cbcc5e5d1c6e28598e8cbbe8-Paper.pdf

15. Schlemper, J., Caballero, J., Hajnal, J.V., Price, A.N., Rueckert, D.: A deep cascade of convolutional neural networks for dynamic MR image reconstruction. IEEE Trans. Med. Imaging **37**(2), 491–503 (2017)
16. Uecker, M., et al.: ESPIRiT - an eigenvalue approach to autocalibrating parallel MRI: where SENSE meets GRAPPA. Mag. Reson. Med. **71**(3), 990–1001 (2014). https://doi.org/10.1002/mrm.24751
17. Wang, P., Chen, E.Z., Chen, T., Patel, V.M., Sun, S.: Pyramid convolutional RNN for MRI reconstruction. arXiv:1912.00543 (2019)
18. Wang, Z., Bovik, A.C., Sheikh, H.R., Simoncelli, E.P.: Image quality assessment: from error visibility to structural similarity. IEEE Trans. Image Process. **13**(4), 600–612 (2004)
19. Yaman, B., Hosseini, S.A.H., Moeller, S., Ellermann, J., Uğurbil, K., Akçakaya, M.: Self-supervised learning of physics-guided reconstruction neural networks without fully sampled reference data. Magn. Reson. Med. **84**(6), 3172–3191 (2020)
20. Yang, G., et al.: DAGAN: deep de-aliasing generative adversarial networks for fast compressed sensing MRI reconstruction. IEEE Trans. Med. Imaging **37**(6), 1310–1321 (2017)
21. Yang, Y., Sun, J., Li, H., Xu, Z.: Deep ADMM-Net for compressive sensing MRI. In: Advances in Neural Information Processing Systems, pp. 10–18 (2016)
22. Yu, S., Park, B., Jeong, J.: Deep iterative down-up CNN for image denoising. In: Proceedings of the IEEE Conference on Computer Vision and Pattern Recognition Workshops (2019)
23. Zbontar, J., et al.: fastMRI: an open dataset and benchmarks for accelerated MRI. arXiv preprint arXiv:1811.08839 (2018)
24. Zhao, H., Gallo, O., Frosio, I., Kautz, J.: Loss functions for neural networks for image processing. arXiv (2015)
25. Zhu, B., Liu, J.Z., Cauley, S.F., Rosen, B.R., Rosen, M.S.: Image reconstruction by domain-transform manifold learning. Nature **555**(7697), 487–492 (2018)

Self-supervised Dynamic MRI Reconstruction

Mert Acar[1,2(✉)], Tolga Çukur[1,2], and İlkay Öksüz[3]

[1] Department of Electrical and Electronics Engineering, Bilkent University,
Ankara, Turkey
mert.acar@bilkent.edu.tr
[2] National Magnetic Resonance Research Center, Bilkent University, Ankara, Turkey
[3] Department of Computer Engineering, Istanbul Technical University,
Istanbul, Turkey

Abstract. Deep learning techniques have recently been adopted for accelerating dynamic MRI acquisitions. Yet, common frameworks for model training rely on availability of large sets of fully-sampled MRI data to construct a ground-truth for the network output. This heavy reliance is undesirable as it is challenging to collect such large datasets in many applications, and even impossible for high spatiotemporal-resolution protocols. In this paper, we introduce self-supervised training to deep neural architectures for dynamic reconstruction of cardiac MRI. We hypothesize that, in the absence of ground-truth data, elevating complexity in self-supervised models can instead constrain model performance due to the deficiencies in training data. To test this working hypothesis, we adopt self-supervised learning on recent state-of-the-art deep models for dynamic MRI, with varying degrees of model complexity. Comparison of supervised and self-supervised variants of deep reconstruction models reveals that compact models have a remarkable advantage in reliability against performance loss in self-supervised settings.

Keywords: Cardiac MRI · Dynamic reconstruction · Self-supervised learning · Convolutional Neural Networks

1 Introduction

Magnetic resonance imaging (MRI) is an extensively utilized modality in routine clinical practice for noninvasive disease detection and monitoring. Dynamic MRI in particular allows in vivo assessment of the moving hearth. Yet, sampling times in dynamic MRI are intrinsically long, only limited data can be captured prior to severe signal decay. This in effect puts restrictions on the spatiotemporal resolution of dynamic cardiac MRI. The common solution to this problem is to reconstruct images from undersampled acquisitions in an effort to maintain desired resolution [4]. Since recollection of missing Fourier coefficients in k-space is an ill-posed problem, prior knowledge on the expected data distribution is needed to guide the reconstructions [6].

© Springer Nature Switzerland AG 2021
N. Haq et al. (Eds.): MLMIR 2021, LNCS 12964, pp. 35–44, 2021.
https://doi.org/10.1007/978-3-030-88552-6_4

In the last decade, compressed sensing (CS) techniques have been a mainstream solution for reconstructing dynamic MRI acquisitions [8,9]. In CS reconstructions, a regularized optimization objective is set up by weighting sparsity priors in known transform domains against fidelity to acquired data samples. The sparsity priors can include both the spatial dimensions (e.g., wavelet coefficients of individual frames), and more critically for dynamic MRI the temporal dimension (e.g., cosine transform coefficients). While CS techniques can shorten scan times in dynamic MRI, compressibility assumptions may be suboptimal in various data domains, and optimization procedures are lengthy [15].

In recent years, deep learning (DL) techniques have come across as a novel solution for reconstruction of accelerated MRI [2,3,10,16]. As opposed to hand-constructed sparsity priors, regularization in DL reconstructions is achieved via a data-driven network model. In this case, the iterative procedures in CS are replaced with a unrolled architecture that interleaves projections through a convolutional neural network with projections to enforce data consistency. For dynamic MRI, recent studies have mostly expressed the reconstruction as a static 2D or 3D problem where frames are independently handled as separate instances [3,13]. The unrolled architecture is trained end-to-end using a large database of fully-sampled MRI data along with corresponding undersampled acquisitions. Supervised learning has produced impressive results to date, however sizable dynamic MRI datasets may not be available in many applications.

The excessive demand for high-quality ground-truth data in supervised learning has sparked interest in self-supervision methods for MRI reconstruction. Promising results have been reported in recent studies for static MRI applications with deep network trained without any access to fully-sampled data [7,17–19]. However, the utility of self-supervision approaches in dynamic cardiac MRI currently remains unknown to the best of our knowledge. The main motivation for the current study is to devise self-supervision strategies in training of deep reconstruction models for dynamic cardiac MRI, given the severely limited number and scope of public datasets on cardiac MRI. Inspired by a recent self-supervision approach for static MRI, here we introduce a self-supervised deep model for dynamic MRI that learns to self-recover subsets of data in readily undersampled acquisitions [18]. To do this, data are split into two nonoverlapping segments in k-space, where the first set is used to enforce data consistency while the second is used to learn network weights.

Supervised deep models of greater complexity are commonly observed to elevate task performance due to their representational capacity [5]. In contrast, we hypothesize that elevating complexity in self-supervised models can instead constrain model performance due to deficiencies in training data. To test this hypothesis, here we implement the proposed self-supervised learning strategy on recent state-of-the-art deep models for dynamic MRI, with varying degrees of complexity. We consider a convolutional recurrent neural network (CRNN) model of low complexity [11], a dynamic reconstruction network (DRN) model of intermediate complexity [5], and a motion-guided DRN (MODRN) model [5] of high complexity. To examine benefits of exploiting temporal correlations, we comparatively demonstrate these models against frame-by-frame reconstructions using a decoupled version of DRN, and a cascade network (CascadeNet) model [13]. Experiments were conducted on a public cardiac MRI dataset [1]. Both supervised and self-supervised variant models were trained. Our results clearly indicate that more compact models can offer increased reliability against performance loss in self-supervised settings compared to complex models.

2 Theory

2.1 Dynamic MRI Reconstruction

Dynamic MRI can be accelerated via undersampling across the phase-encoding dimension. Let the temporal sequence of fully-sampled, complex MR images is denoted as $\{\mathbf{x}_t\}_{t\in\tau} \in \mathbb{C}^N$ where each 2D frame is cast into a column vector across spatial dimensions of length $N = N_x N_y$ and τ is the number of frames. Reconstruction can be achieved by recovering $\{\mathbf{x}_t\}_{t\in\tau}$ from an set of undersampled k-space measurements $\{\mathbf{y}_t\}_{t\in\tau} \in \mathbb{C}^K (K \ll N)$ such that:

$$\mathbf{y}_t = \mathbf{F}_u \mathbf{x}_t + \mathbf{e} \tag{1}$$

where $\mathbf{F}_u$ is the partial Fourier encoding operator and $\mathbf{e} \in \mathbb{C}^K$ denotes measurement noise. As undersampled acquisitions violate the Nyquist condition, Eq. 1 is underdetermined and therefore its solutions benefits from prior information. Prior knowledge can be incorporated as a regularization term:

$$\mathscr{L}_{rec}(\{\mathbf{x}_t\}) = \sum_{t=1}^{\tau} (\mathscr{R}(\mathbf{x}_t) + \lambda \|\mathbf{F}_u \mathbf{x}_t - \mathbf{y}_t\|_2^2) \tag{2}$$

In Eq. 2 $\mathscr{R}$ stands for the regularization term imposed on $\mathbf{x}$, and $\lambda \in \mathbb{R}$ s the relative weighting of the data fidelity term against the regularizer. In DL-based reconstruction, regularization is achieved via mapping through a convolutional neural network (CNN) to map undersampled data to fully-sampled images:

$$\mathscr{L}_{rec}(\{\mathbf{x}_t\}) = \sum_{t=1}^{\tau} (\|\mathbf{x}_t - \mathscr{F}_{cnn}(\mathbf{x}_{t_u}|\theta)\|_2^2 + \lambda \|\mathbf{F}_u \mathbf{x}_t - \mathbf{y}_t\|_2^2) \tag{3}$$

where $\mathscr{F}_{cnn}(.|\theta)$ is the CNN mapping characterized by the parameter vector θ, $\mathbf{x}_{t_u} = \mathbf{F}_u^H \mathbf{y}_t$. Note that $\mathbf{F}_u^H$ denotes the Hermitian of the Fourier operator.

The quality of the reconstructed image is affected heavily by the internal structure of the function $\mathscr{F}_{cnn}(.|\theta)$, which represents the architecture of the underlying network. As a common design choice across all of the experimented architectures, the regularization is done in cascaded CNN iterations interleaved with Data Consistency (DC) modules proposed in [13], which enforces the data fidelity of the already-sampled k-space points denoted with the set Ω. While the solution uses the predicted values from CNN iterations for the unknown k-space samples (i.e. $i \notin \Omega$), for the already-sampled entries (i.e. $i \in \Omega$) we take the noise-weighted linear combination of the predictions and the acquired samples. For the interpolated k-space output from the CNN layer $\{\mathbf{m}_t\}_{cnn} = \mathbf{F}\{\mathbf{x}_t\}_{cnn} = \mathbf{F}\mathscr{F}_{cnn}(\mathbf{x}_{t_u}|\theta)$:

$$DC(\{\mathbf{m}_t\}_{cnn}) = \begin{cases} \{\mathbf{m}_t\}_{cnn}(i) & \text{if } i \notin \Omega \\ \frac{\{\mathbf{m}_t\}_{cnn}(i)+\mu\{\mathbf{m}_t\}_0(i)}{1+\mu} & \text{if } i \in \Omega \end{cases} \tag{4}$$

where $\{\mathbf{m}_t\}_0$ is the zero-filled k-space obtained from the zero-filled complex-valued image $\{\mathbf{m}_t\}_0 = \mathbf{F}\mathbf{F}_u^H \mathbf{y}_t$. Here the parameter μ is inversely proportional to the noise power in the acquisitions. It can be seen that in the limit $\mu \to \infty$ the data-consistency operator converges to strict data fidelity [14].

2.2   Self-supervised Learning

As discussed previously, fully-sampled acquisitions in dynamic cardiac imaging are often difficult to collect due to motion, signal decay, and long scan times. To address associated challenges in training neural networks, we introduce a self-supervised learning strategy for dynamic MRI reconstructions inspired by [18]. In this strategy, a subset of k-space data in undersampled MR acquisitions is masked out, and the network is trained to predict the masked samples from non-masked samples. Thus, the network weights are optimized to minimize the prediction error for masked samples, in an effort to prevent reliance on fully-sampled ground truth. Assuming the superset of acquired k-space samples is Ω, this superset is split into to non-overlapping subsets as follows:

$$\Omega = \Theta \cup \Lambda \tag{5}$$

The set Θ is used in the data consistency operation during training to enforce fidelity whereas the set Λ is used to define the loss function in k-space:

$$\min_\theta \mathscr{L}(\mathbf{m}_\Lambda, \mathbf{m}_{cnn_\Lambda}|\theta)) \tag{6}$$

where θ is the set of trainable network parameters, $\mathbf{m}_\Lambda$ are acquired k-space samples in Λ pooled across all frames, and $\mathbf{m}_{cnn_\Lambda}$ are reconstructed k-space samples in Λ. The optimization objective is to minimize the discrepancy between reconstructed and acquired k-space data. Meanwhile, data consistency operations are only performed for k-space samples in Θ. Here the loss function is taken as normalized $\ell_1 - \ell_2$ loss:

$$\mathscr{L}(\mathbf{m}, \mathbf{m}_{cnn}) = \sum_{t=1}^{\tau} \frac{\|\mathbf{m}_t - \mathbf{m}_{t_{cnn}}\|_2}{\|\mathbf{m}_t\|_2} + \frac{\|\mathbf{m}_t - \mathbf{m}_{t_{cnn}}\|_1}{\|\mathbf{m}_t\|_1} \tag{7}$$

where during supervised training $\mathbf{m}$ and $\mathbf{m}_{cnn}$ correspond to the reference fully-sampled cine series in k-space and the network output in k-space respectively. In the case of self-supervised training, these refer to k-space samples with index Λ from the measurements and the network output respectively.

The success of the self-supervision strategy considered in this study relies on the resulting model's ability to generalize across varying subsets of acquired and missing k-space samples.

3   Methods

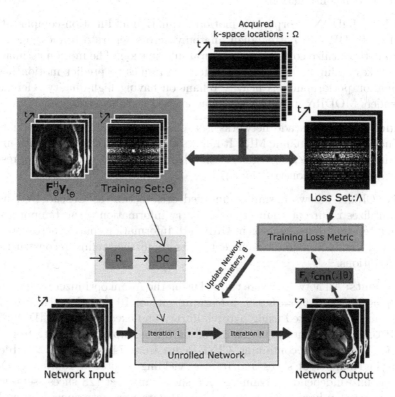

Fig. 1. The self-supervised training strategy adapted to an unrolled network architecture for dynamic MRI reconstructions.

Self-supervision alleviates the harsh data requirements of supervised learning for deep neural networks architectures with thousands-to-millions of parameters. However, training models on inherently lower-quality undersampled acquisitions might slow down learning procedures. Here, we hypothesized that self-supervised models would require greater amount of data for training, and so this would give a performance advantage to more compact models with fewer parameters over large models. To test this hypothesis, we evaluated several state-of-the-art deep architectures for dynamic MRI reconstruction in both supervised and self-supervised settings using the structure shown in Fig. 1. Critically, we experimented with architectures of varying orders of model complexity. All architectures were trained to solve Eq. 3 by alternating between network-driven regularization and data consistency blocks.

DRN: The dynamic reconstruction network is based on a U-Net backbone [12] with recurrent modules to exploit redundancies in temporal and unrolling dimensions [5]. Here, we considered two variants of DRN models: a static 2D-DRN model that independently reconstructed each individual frame, and an aggregate DRN model that reconstructed all frames concurrently. A comparison among these variants allowed us to assess potential benefits of temporal correlations in dynamic MRI reconstruction.

MODRN: MODRN incorporates motion-estimation and motion-compensation networks into DRN to better align anatomy across separate frames [5], in an effort to better utilize correlated structural information. The motion estimation module takes as input fully-sampled reference frames to predict motion fields, as estimation performance is heavily reliant on having high-quality references. This renders MODRN unsuited to self-supervised learning strategies.

CascadeNet: The cascade networks is a baseline for static reconstruction of individual frames in dynamic MRI. It follows an unrolled architecture with interleaved data consistency and regularization blocks, and progressively suppressed aliasing artifacts in reconstructions [13].

CRNN: CRNN follows a similar unrolled architecture as CascadeNet, however, it utilizes recurrent connections to carry information along temporal and unrolling iteration dimensions as in DRN [11]. Information sharing across frames is achieved via bidirectional recurrent units to further refine reconstructions across iterations.

Experiments: All networks were trained using the Adam optimizer with parameters $\beta_1 = 0.99$ and $\beta_2 = 0.999$, a learning rate of 10^{-4} and batch size of 1. Models were implemented using pytorch library and executed on NVIDIA RTX 3090 GPUs. Experiments were conducted on fully-sampled MRI data from the public OCMR dataset containing CINE scans from 74 subjects [1]. Subjects had varying number of slices and frames, yielding a total of 183 slices. Data were split into independent training (155 slices) and test (28 slices) sets, with no subject overlap between the two sets. MRI data were retrospectively undersampled to achieve acceleration rates of 4 and 8. A Gaussian sampling density with an autocalibration region containing 8 lines was used. For self-supervised learning, acquired k-space was split into two distinct sets at ratio 3:2 [18]. Reconstruction quality was assessed by measuring peak signal-to-noise ratio (PSNR), structural similarity index (SSIM) and mean-squared error (MSE) between the reconstructed and ground-truth images.

4   Experimental Results

Figure 2 illustrates reconstructions in a representative test subject at 4× and 8× acceleration along with fully-sampled ground truth. PSNR, SSIM and MSE of all tested methods are presented in Tables 1 and 2, along with the embodied number of model parameters. While the supervised MODRN model with the

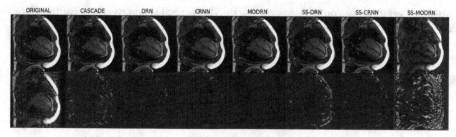

(a) x4 Acceleration

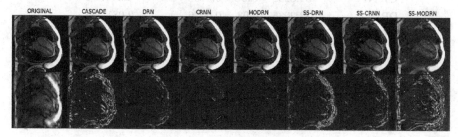

(b) x8 Acceleration

Fig. 2. Representative reconstructions from competing architectures at (a) 4-fold, (b) 8-fold acceleration. The first column displays Fourier reconstructions of fully-sampled and undersampled data. In remaining columns, the second row shows error maps for each architecture. The prefix 'SS' denotes a model trained via self supervision.

greatest model complexity exhibits the highest performance, its self-supervised variant suffers heavily in the absence of fully-sampled reference data. Note that MODRN learns to create motion flow maps between the current frame being reconstructed and two reference frames marking a predetermined period T in the time axis. When supplied with undersampled frames, the estimated motion maps fail to capture anatomical motion due to undersampling artifacts greatly changing from frame to frame dominating the motion flow maps. Divorced of the motion estimation and compensation units, DRN offers somewhat lower performance for an order of magnitude fewer parameters. As it does not take any fully-sampled reference inputs, its deterioration in self-supervision is relatively lower. The static 2D-DRN and CascadeNet models naturally deteriorate around high-motion areas, and yield the poorest performances. Lastly, the compact CRNN model maintains on par performance to the MODRN model in the supervised setting, despite having two orders of magnitude fewer parameters. Furthermore, CRNN is able to maintain its performance reliably even in self-supervised setting. These results indicate that learning network models with self supervision increases data demands, since reference data are undersampled in this case. Therefore, compact network models have a remarkable edge for successful training via self supervision.

Table 1. Performance comparisons (MSE, PSNR and SSIM) on dynamic cardiac data with ×4 acceleration rate across experiment setups. MSE is scaled with 10^3. Self-supervised schemes have 'SS' prefix while static reconstruction settings are indicated by '2D' suffix.

Method	PSNR	SSIM	MSE ($\times 10^{-3}$)	Complexity
Supervised training (×4)				
2D-DRN	28.3257	0.89	0.0294	2,081,250
CascadeNet	31.6621	0.92	0.0158	678,924
CRNN	34.8252	**0.95**	0.0105	**297,794**
DRN	33.2935	0.93	0.0076	2,081,250
MODRN	**35.4119**	**0.95**	**0.0044**	21,198,822
Self-supervised training (×4)				
SS-CascadeNet	27.2024	0.86	0.0388	678,924
SS-CRNN	**33.6359**	**0.93**	**0.0069**	**297,794**
SS-DRN	31.8702	0.93	0.0151	2,081,250
SS-MODRN	22.7439	0.78	0.1264	21,198,822

Table 2. Performance comparisons (MSE, PSNR and SSIM) on dynamic cardiac data with x8 acceleration rate across experiment setups. MSE is scaled with 10^3. Self-supervised schemes have 'SS' prefix while static reconstruction settings are indicated by '2D' suffix.

Method	PSNR	SSIM	MSE ($\times 10^{-3}$)	Complexity
Supervised training (×8)				
2D-DRN	22.5123	0.81	0.0922	2,081,250
CascadeNet	26.0021	0.85	0.0592	678,924
CRNN	32.9124	**0.92**	0.0094	**297,794**
DRN	31.2637	0.91	0.0178	2,081,250
MODRN	**33.4434**	**0.92**	**0.0071**	21,198,822
Self-supervised training (×8)				
SS-CascadeNet	24.2161	0.81	0.0888	678,924
SS-CRNN	**30.1501**	**0.91**	**0.0213**	**297,794**
SS-DRN	28.1245	0.88	0.0419	2,081,250
SS-MODRN	16.6932	0.65	0.4244	21,198,822

5   Conclusion

Here we introduced a self-supervision approach to deep reconstruction networks for dynamic cardiac MRI acquisitions. Experiments were conducted to systematically evaluate the amenability of models of varying complexity to self supervision. Our results indicate that a compact unrolled CNN architecture with bidirectional recurrent connections exhibits robustness against lowered quality of training data in self-supervised learning, and achieves on par performance with supervised duals.

Acknowledgments. This paper has been produced benefiting from the 2232 International Fellowship for Outstanding Researchers Program of TUBITAK (Project No: 118C353). However, the entire responsibility of the publication/paper belongs to the owner of the paper. The financial support received from TUBITAK does not mean that the content of the publication is approved in a scientific sense by TUBITAK.

References

1. Chen, C., et al.: OCMR (v1.0)-open-access multi-coil k-space dataset for cardiovascular magnetic resonance imaging (2020)
2. Dar, S.U., Yurt, M., Shahdloo, M., Ildız, M.E., Tınaz, B., Çukur, T.: Prior-guided image reconstruction for accelerated multi-contrast MRI via generative adversarial networks. IEEE J. Sel. Top. Signal Process. **14**(6), 1072–1087 (2020). https://doi.org/10.1109/JSTSP.2020.3001737
3. Fuin, N., et al.: A multi-scale variational neural network for accelerating motion-compensated whole-heart 3d coronary MR angiography. Magn. Reson. Imaging **70**, 155–167 (2020). https://doi.org/10.1016/j.mri.2020.04.007. https://www.sciencedirect.com/science/article/pii/S0730725X1930671X
4. Gamper, U., Boesiger, P., Kozerke, S.: Compressed sensing in dynamic MRI. Magn. Reson. Med. **59**(2), 365–373 (2008). https://doi.org/10.1002/mrm.21477. https://onlinelibrary.wiley.com/doi/abs/10.1002/mrm.21477
5. Huang, Q., et al.: Dynamic MRI reconstruction with end-to-end motion-guided network. Med. Image Anal. **68**, 101901 (2021). https://doi.org/10.1016/j.media.2020.101901. https://www.sciencedirect.com/science/article/pii/S1361841520302656
6. Jung, H., Sung, K., Nayak, K.S., Kim, E.Y., Ye, J.C.: K-T focuss: a general compressed sensing framework for high resolution dynamic MRI. Magn. Reson. Med. **61**(1), 103–116 (2009). https://doi.org/10.1002/mrm.21757
7. Korkmaz, Y., Dar, S.U., Yurt, M., Özbey, M., Çukur, T.: Unsupervised MRI reconstruction via zero-shot learned adversarial transformers (2021)
8. Lingala, S.G., DiBella, E., Jacob, M.: Deformation corrected compressed sensing (DC-CS): a novel framework for accelerated dynamic MRI. IEEE Trans. Med. Imaging **34**(1), 72–85 (2015). https://doi.org/10.1109/TMI.2014.2343953
9. Majumdar, A., Ward, R.K., Aboulnasr, T.: Compressed sensing based real-time dynamic MRI reconstruction. IEEE Trans. Med. Imaging **31**(12), 2253–2266 (2012). https://doi.org/10.1109/TMI.2012.2215921
10. Oksuz, I., et al.: Cardiac MR motion artefact correction from K-space using deep learning-based reconstruction. In: Knoll, F., Maier, A., Rueckert, D. (eds.) MLMIR 2018. LNCS, vol. 11074, pp. 21–29. Springer, Cham (2018). https://doi.org/10.1007/978-3-030-00129-2_3
11. Qin, C., Schlemper, J., Caballero, J., Price, A., Hajnal, J.V., Rueckert, D.: Convolutional recurrent neural networks for dynamic MR image reconstruction (2018)
12. Ronneberger, O., Fischer, P., Brox, T.: U-Net: convolutional networks for biomedical image segmentation. In: Navab, N., Hornegger, J., Wells, W.M., Frangi, A.F. (eds.) MICCAI 2015. LNCS, vol. 9351, pp. 234–241. Springer, Cham (2015). https://doi.org/10.1007/978-3-319-24574-4_28

13. Schlemper, J., Caballero, J., Hajnal, J.V., Price, A., Rueckert, D.: A deep cascade of convolutional neural networks for MR image reconstruction. In: Niethammer, M., et al. (eds.) IPMI 2017. LNCS, vol. 10265, pp. 647–658. Springer, Cham (2017). https://doi.org/10.1007/978-3-319-59050-9_51

14. Schlemper, J., Caballero, J., Hajnal, J.V., Price, A.N., Rueckert, D.: A deep cascade of convolutional neural networks for dynamic MR image reconstruction. IEEE Trans. Med. Imaging **37**(2), 491–503 (2018). https://doi.org/10.1109/TMI.2017.2760978

15. Shahdloo, M., Ilicak, E., Tofighi, M., Saritas, E.U., Çetin, A.E., Çukur, T.: Projection onto epigraph sets for rapid self-tuning compressed sensing MRI. IEEE Trans. Med. Imaging **38**(7), 1677–1689 (2019). https://doi.org/10.1109/TMI.2018.2885599

16. Wang, S., et al.: Accelerating magnetic resonance imaging via deep learning. In: 2016 IEEE 13th International Symposium on Biomedical Imaging (ISBI), pp. 514–517 (2016). https://doi.org/10.1109/ISBI.2016.7493320

17. Yaman, B., Hosseini, S.A.H., Akçakaya, M.: Zero-shot self-supervised learning for MRI reconstruction (2021)

18. Yaman, B., Hosseini, S.A.H., Moeller, S., Ellermann, J., Uğurbil, K., Akçakaya, M.: Self-supervised learning of physics-guided reconstruction neural networks without fully sampled reference data. Magnetic Resonance in Medicine **84**(6), 3172–3191 (2020). https://doi.org/10.1002/mrm.28378. http://dx.doi.org/10.1002/mrm.28378

19. Yaman, B., Shenoy, C., Deng, Z., Moeller, S., El-Rewaidy, H., Nezafat, R., Akçakaya, M.: Self-supervised physics-guided deep learning reconstruction for high-resolution 3d lge cmr. In: 2021 IEEE 18th International Symposium on Biomedical Imaging (ISBI). pp. 100–104 (2021). https://doi.org/10.1109/ISBI48211.2021.9434054

A Simulation Pipeline to Generate Realistic Breast Images for Learning DCE-MRI Reconstruction

Zhengnan Huang[1,2(✉)], Jonghyun Bae[1,2,3], Patricia M. Johnson[2],
Terlika Sood[2], Laura Heacock[2], Justin Fogarty[2], Linda Moy[1,2],
Sungheon Gene Kim[2,3], and Florian Knoll[2]

[1] Vilcek Institute of Graduate Biomedical Sciences, New York University School
of Medicine, New York, USA
zh1115@nyu.edu
[2] Center for Biomedical Imaging, Radiology, New York University School
of Medicine, New York, USA
[3] Department of Radiology, Weill Cornell Medical College, New York, USA

Abstract. Dynamic contrast enhancement (DCE) MRI has been
increasingly utilized in clinical practice. While machine learning (ML)
applications are gaining momentum in MRI reconstruction, the dynamic
nature of image acquisition for DCE-MRI limits access to a simultaneously high spatial and temporal resolution ground truth image for supervised ML applications. In this study, we introduced a pipeline to simulate the ground truth DCE-MRI k-space data from real breast perfusion
images. Based on physical model and the clinical images, we estimate the
perfusion parameters. Treating those as ground truth, we simulated the
signal. Using our simulated images, we trained ML reconstruction models. We demonstrate the utility of our simulation pipeline using two ML
models and one conventional reconstruction method. Our results suggest
that, even though the image quality of the ML reconstructions seem to
be very close to the simulated ground truth, the temporal pattern and
its kinetic parameters may not be close to the ground truth data.

Keywords: DCE-MRI · Machine learning · Reconstruction

1 Introduction

Supervised machine learning relies heavily on high quality training data. As an
innovative technique for MRI reconstruction, ML reconstruction has shown its
capability to increase the acceleration factor and shorten the scan time without
sacrificing the image quality [1]. Unlike conventional reconstruction methods
[2–4], ML reconstruction requires ground truth images as training data. When
fully sampled k-space data can be acquired, it is easy to obtain a high quality

Z. Huang and J. Bae—Equal contribution.

ground truth image. An under-sampled k-space can be also easily simulated by retrospectively undersampling the ground truth data. This is then used to train ML models to reconstruct images from under-sampled k-space data.

For DCE-MRI, high spatial and temporal resolution image cannot be obtained simultaneously in most cases. With current techniques [6,7], there is an inherent trade-off between acquiring an image with high spatial or high temporal resolution. This limits our capability to evaluate both the spatial features and contrast uptake temporal features in breast tissue and ultimately our ability to classify lesions.

In this project, we developed a simulation platform to generate ground truth dynamic contrast enhanced images based on GRASP [6] breast DCE-MR images and the tissue contrast kinetic parameters estimated using the two compartment model (TCM) [5]. This platform was used to achieve both realistic pixel-wise contrast dynamics relevant to lesions as well as normal tissues including the fibroglandular tissue, muscle and the heart. We trained two ML models with these simulated images and k-space data. Our main goal was to establish this simulation pipeline as a tool to develop as well as evaluate ML reconstruction methods for dynamic imaging by enabling comparisons between the reconstructed images and the simulated ground truth images.

2 Method

2.1 DCE-MRI Data Acquisition

To establish a realistic simulation pipeline, we used breast DCE-MRI data collected through an institutional review board approved HIPPA compliant retrospective study (study number S18-00684). Breast perfusion images from 61 patients were evaluated. Of these patients, 24 had a malignant lesion and 37 had a benign lesion. A whole body 3T MRI scanner (MAGNETOM, TimTrio, Siemens Healthcare, Erlangen, Germany) with a 16-channel breast coil (In vivo, Orlando, FL) was used to acquire data for all patients. Golden-angle spoke ordering radial stack-of-star 3D spoiled gradient echo sequence was used [6,7]. Each scan generates 288 spokes with 83 partitions for 2.5 min. Scan parameters were: TE = 1.80 ms, TR = 4.87 ms, flip angle = 10°, FOV = 320 × 320 × 212 mm^3 and axial slab orientation. The spatial resolution is 1.0 × 1.0 × 1.1 mm. The image size was 320 × 320.

To differentiate the tissues with different vascular permeabilities, which is critical in distinguishing normal fibroglandular breast tissue, benign and malignant lesions, we used Gadolinium-Based contrast agent (GBCA). The imaging protocol includes a 60-s baseline acquisition with no contrast agent, followed by contrast injection and continuing to scan for the remaining 90 s scan. Gadobutrol (Gadavist, Bayer Healthcare Pharmaceuticals) was injected (0.1 mmol/kg body weight) at a speed of 2 mL/s.

The images were reconstructed using GRASP [6]. Coil sensitivities were calculated by dividing the coil images with 'sum-of-squares' image [3]. This approach can be replaced by other sensitivities estimation techniques. For the base image of our simulation, we selected a single slice from a 3D volume such that the selected image slice shows a lesion.

2.2   Pharmacokinetics Model Analysis and Simulation

Vascular and cellular microstructural properties could be described by Pharmacokinetic model parameters. Pharmacokinetic model (PKM) analysis was performed to estimate pixel-wise perfusion parameters [8]. We used the Two Compartment Exchange Model (TCM), that has four parameters, namely v_e, v_p, plasma perfusion (F_p) and vascular endothelial permeability-surface area product (PS). v_e is the volume fraction of extracellular-extravascular space. v_p is the blood plasma compartment volume fraction. F_p is the blood plasma flow from the artery to the tissue capillary bed. PS is the bidirectional endothelial permeability-surface product. Another crucial data, the artery input function (AIF), was extracted from a region of interest in the aorta. Those parameters were used to generate ground truth images in our simulation.

We manually segmented the image into 6 regions: breast lesion (including benign and malignant ones), fibroglandular tissue, muscle, skin, heart and liver. Different T1 values were assigned to those tissues, based on the literature values, in order to model the T1 shorting effect of the GBCA. For a given AIF, T1 and pharmacokinetic parameters, we used TCM to simulate the time signal enhancement curve. Using the time signal enhancement curves of different regions and a pre-contrast image, we generate dynamic contrast enhanced images. This workflow is illustrated in Fig. 1.

2.3   MR Acquisition Simulation

To simulate the radial acquisition for DCE-MRI, we used the open source platform torchkbnufft [9] for Non-Uniform Fast Fourier Transform (NUFFT) [10]. Coil sensitivities estimated during the reconstruction of real breast DCE-MRI data were used for simulation of the multi-coil receiver system. After applying coil sensitivities to the dynamic image to simulate individual coil images, NUFFT was performed to transform the coil images to radial k-space data. Each radial k-space readout line (spoke) had 640 sampling points. In each temporal frame, data for 21 spokes were generated to simulate an under-sampled scan. For our simulated DCE-MRI series of dimension $320 \times 320 \times 22$, the simulation generates under-sampled radial kspace of size $16 \times 640 \times 21 \times 22$, where the first dimension is the coil dimension. To meet Nyquist sampling rate, $\frac{320\pi}{2} \approx 503$ spokes are needed for each frame. Our 21 spokes simulation corresponds to an acceleration factor of 24. The Cartesian k-space simulation is straight forward by using FFT. Random under-sampling was perform to acquire the zero-filled k-space according to the published CRNN code [11], where a zero-mean Gaussian distribution was used to generate the sampling mask with more frequent samples in the low spacial frequency part of the k-space [12]. In this experiment, we set the acceleration factor to 4 for Cartesian k-space. For the purpose of observing the performance of the ML reconstruction without the interference of noise, no noise was added to the simulated image or the k-space data.

2.4   Testing with ML Reconstruction

We tested the established DCE-MRI simulation pipeline with 2 ML reconstruction methods. One was our own unrolled iterative ML reconstruction prototype (ML1). The model has 28 gradient descent stages. Each stage has a data consistency part and a regularization part. Mean square error (MSE) loss of the reconstruction was combined with the MSE loss of the relevant signal enhancement to train the model. The relevant enhancement was calculated by dividing the average baseline signal (average signal from the first 5 frames). Another reconstruction technique is CRNN from [11] which reconstructs image from Cartesian k-space. It has a bi-directional convolutional and recurrent neural network as regularizer, formulated in a more complex way than ML1, allowing information and gradient flow between iterative stages and temporal frames.

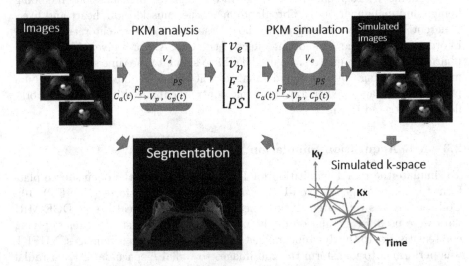

Fig. 1. GRASP images were used as the base of the simulation. First the PKM analysis was performed to extract the perfusion parameters. Manual segmentation information and the perfusion parameters were used for the contrast enhancement simulation. Applying the contrast enhancement to the static (pre-contrast) image generated the simulated image time series. k-space of different sampling trajectory (showing only radial trajectory) of the simulated image can be generated for reconstruction model training.

The DCE-MRI images generated by the simulation pipeline were randomly split into training (51), validation (5) and test (5) sets. The testing set was set aside for final evaluation of ML models after training and validation. Note this experiment does not serve as a comparison between different reconstruction

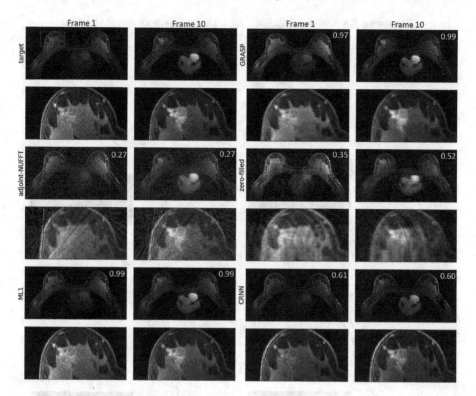

Fig. 2. Left 2 columns from top to bottom are: 1. simulated target, 2. adjoint-NUFFT of the radial kspace, 3. ML1 reconstruction from radial kspace. Right 2 column from top to bottom: 1. GRASP reconstruction from radial kspace. 2. zero filled reconstruction from Cartesian kspace. 3. CRNN reconstruction from radial kspace. The columns are the 1st, 10th frame from the image time series. Each row is followed by the zoom-in view of the benign lesion in the right breast of the patient (left side in the picture) The acceleration factor is 4 for the reconstruction and 24 for our Radial k-space reconstruction. Structural similarity was calculated and marked on each image

methods, but an assessment of the practicality of our simulation pipeline in ML-based image reconstruction research.

3   Result

The data generated by the simulation pipeline were successfully used to train and assess various reconstruction methods. The images from ML reconstruction methods suggest that good visual quality can be achieved with the simulated data. Example image results are shown in Fig. 2. The tumor from the trained reconstruction has more defined margins (Fig. 2, bottom row), when compared to the lesion in the GRASP reconstructed images. The ML1 reconstruction also generated higher structure similarity. The CRNN model generated images with some

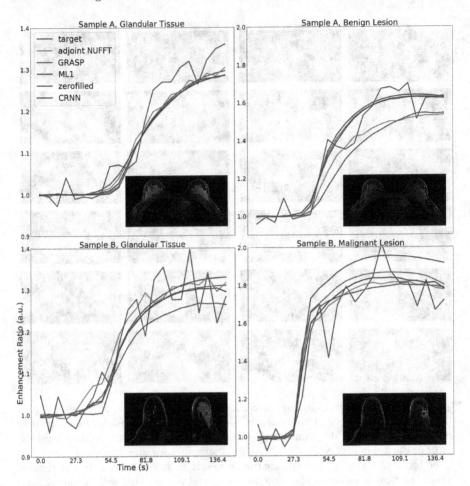

Fig. 3. Four subplots are the averaged signal enhancement ratio within 4 different ROIs (specified in the subplot title) from the simulated ground truth and the reconstruction images. Enhancement ratio is the ratio between the signal intensity and the averaged baseline (pre-contrast) signal intensity. The corresponding ROIs are shown in the lower right corner of each subplot. Note the two subplots on the right has different y-axis scale then the two subplots on the left.

structure incorrectly enhanced, (Fig. 2, bottom row, right 2 columns) suggesting more iterations and hyper-parameter tuning might be required. The incorrect anatomical structure might be the cause of the low SSIM of this CRNN reconstructed image. The images shown in Fig. 2 demonstrate that the spatial quality of the reconstructed images can be assessed against the ground truth images.

In addition to the spatial fidelity, the simulation pipeline allows to assess the temporal fidelity of the reconstructed images, as shown in Fig. 3. The averaged relative enhancement curves from the lesion ROIs show significant differences from the curve of the simulated target, as shown in Fig. 3. The ML1 reconstruction curve suffered substantially from smoothing and reduced relative enhancement. Averaged signal curves from GRASP reconstruction showed better visual alignment with the ground truth curves. Further quantitative evaluation by the pharmacokinetic analysis showed that the PS estimated from the ML reconstruction was inaccurate. This is illustrated in Fig. 4.

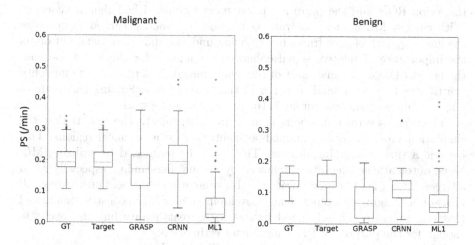

Fig. 4. Distribution of simulated ground truth PS and PS from PKM analysis using the simulated target, GRASP reconstruction, CRNN reconstruction and ML1 reconstruction. 'GT' stands for the ground truth perfusion parameters we used for the simulation. 'Target' is the estimated parameters using the simulated ground truth image. Left and right subplot are the results from one malignant and one benign lesion respectively in the validation set

4   Discussion

Deep learning has been widely applied and tested in MR image reconstruction. However, it remains challenging to find an accurate ground truth image to train ML reconstruction for DCE-MRI. An accurate ground truth will also enable quantitative evaluation of the dynamic curves, which is crucial for the purpose of PKM analysis and downstream applications. For ML reconstruction itself, one of the important questions is whether an adequate convergence can be achieved during training [13]. Previously, we have attempted to use GRASP reconstructed images from under-sampled radial k-space as the ground truth. The ML reconstruction trained with such ground truth would not likely outperform the conventional reconstruction used as the ground truth. It was also uncertain whether the ML reconstruction that performs well in terms of MSE, SSIM and visual assessment converged to a physically accurate time series.

To address these problems, we developed this pipeline to simulate realistic ground truth images with signal dynamics defined by the two compartment exchange model and its parameters. As demonstrated in this study, the proposed simulation pipeline can be used to train ML reconstruction models with high temporal and spatial resolution ground truth for DCE-MRI.

With such ground truth, we were able to experiment with two ML reconstruction models. Both models reconstructed images of good visual quality. One model showed high structural similarity. However, the comparison between the learned reconstruction and ground truth showed that the averaged signal from the lesion ROIs and the perfusion parameters estimated had significant error. With current ML model and training method, the model learned to optimize the image quality of each frame by removing undersampling artifacts, but omits the importance of relative signal enhancement fidelity for the lesion. Because the lesion ROIs are a small part of the whole image. It is possible the infidelity contributes only to a small fraction of the training loss. Solving this issue of relative enhancement inaccuracy is the focus of ongoing work.

There are several limitations to note in this project. The first is that the simulation process requires manual segmentation for anatomical regions. This became a time consuming process. This could be addressed by utilizing ML-based automatic segmentation, followed by manual fine-tuning, especially when a larger dataset is to be incorporated in this simulation pipeline. Future work will focus on leveraging this pipeline and developing a new ML reconstruction model that can generate not only good images with great quality but also accurate enough for the purpose of PKM parameter estimation.

The source code used in this project can be shared upon reasonable request.

5   Conclusion

We successfully developed a simulation pipeline for training and evaluating ML-based DCE-MRI reconstruction methods. Two ML models were trained using this simulation pipeline to demonstrate the utility of the simulation pipeline. The results showed that the reconstructed image quality from one ML model was satisfactory, but its time-signal enhancement curve was not accurate enough for PKM analysis to generate perfusion parameters. This simulation pipeline showed the physical inaccuracy of the ML reconstruction when acceleration is high. With traditional MSE loss, ML models might produce a reconstruction with both high SSIM and good visual image quality. But the signal level fidelity might still be lost during the training process. This issue need to be addressed when downstream application of the reconstruction involves quantitative analysis, for instance, PKM analysis.

References

1. Hammernik, K., Klatzer, T., Kobler, E., et al.: Learning a variational network for reconstruction of accelerated MRI data. Magn. Reson. Med. **79**(6), 3055–3071 (2018)
2. Sodickson, D.K., Manning, W.J.: Simultaneous acquisition of spatial harmonics (SMASH): fast imaging with radiofrequency coil arrays. Magn. Reson. Med. **38**(4), 591–603 (1997)
3. Pruessmann, K.P., Weiger, M., Scheidegger, M.B., Boesiger, P.: SENSE: sensitivity encoding for fast MRI. Magn. Reson. Med. **42**(5), 952–962 (1999)
4. Griswold, M.A., Jakob, P.M., Heidemann, R.M., et al.: Generalized autocalibrating partially parallel acquisitions (GRAPPA). Magn. Reson. Med. **47**(6), 1202–1210 (2002)
5. Sourbron, S.P., Buckley, D.L.: Tracer kinetic modelling in MRI: estimating perfusion and capillary permeability. Phys. Med. Biol. **57**(2), R1–R33 (2012)
6. Feng, L., Grimm, R., Block, K.T., et al.: Golden-angle radial sparse parallel MRI: combination of compressed sensing, parallel imaging, and golden-angle radial sampling for fast and flexible dynamic volumetric MRI. Magn. Reson. Med. **72**(3), 707–717 (2014)
7. Kim, S.G., Feng, L., Grimm, R., et al.: Influence of temporal regularization and radial undersampling factor on compressed sensing reconstruction in dynamic contrast enhanced MRI of the breast. J. Magn. Reson. Imaging **43**(1), 261–269 (2016)
8. Kim, S.G., Freed, M., Leite, A.P.K., Zhang, J., Seuss, C., Moy, L.: Separation of benign and malignant breast lesions using dynamic contrast enhanced MRI in a biopsy cohort. J. Magn. Reson. Imaging **45**(5), 1385–1393 (2017)
9. Muckley, J.M., Stern, R., Murrell, T., Knoll, F.: TorchKbNufft: a high-level, hardware-agnostic non-uniform fast Fourier transform. In: ISMRM Workshop on Data Sampling and Image Reconstruction (2020)
10. Fessler, J.A., Sutton, B.P.: Nonuniform fast Fourier transforms using min-max interpolation. IEEE Trans. Sig. Process. **51**(2), 560–574 (2003). https://doi.org/10.1109/TSP.2002.807005
11. Qin, C., Schlemper, J., Caballero, J., Price, A.N., Hajnal, J.V., Rueckert, D.: Convolutional recurrent neural networks for dynamic MR image reconstruction. IEEE Trans. Med. Imaging **38**(1), 280–290 (2019). https://doi.org/10.1109/TMI.2018.2863670
12. Jung, H., Ye, J.C., Kim, E.Y.: Improved k-t BLAST and k-t SENSE using FOCUSS. Phys. Med. Biol. **52**(11), 3201–3226 (2007)
13. Antun, V., Colbrook, M.J., Hansen, A.: Can stable and accurate neural networks be computed? - on the barriers of deep learning and Smale's 18th problem. ArXiv, abs/2101.08286 (2021)

Deep MRI Reconstruction with Generative Vision Transformers

Yilmaz Korkmaz[1,2], Mahmut Yurt[1,2], Salman Ul Hassan Dar[1,2],
Muzaffer Özbey[1,2], and Tolga Cukur[1,2(✉)]

[1] Department of Electrical and Electronics Engineering, Bilkent University,
Ankara, Turkey
cukur@ee.bilkent.edu.tr
[2] National Magnetic Resonance Research Center (UMRAM), Bilkent University,
Ankara, Turkey

Abstract. Supervised training of deep network models for MRI reconstruction requires access to large databases of fully-sampled MRI acquisitions. To alleviate dependency on costly databases, unsupervised learning strategies have received interest. A powerful framework that eliminates the need for training data altogether is the deep image prior (DIP). To do this, DIP inverts randomly-initialized models to infer network parameters most consistent with the undersampled test data. However, existing DIP methods leverage convolutional backbones, suffering from limited sensitivity to long-range spatial dependencies and thereby poor model invertibility. To address these limitations, here we propose an unsupervised MRI reconstruction based on a novel generative vision transformer (GVTrans). GVTrans progressively maps low-dimensional noise and latent variables onto MR images via cascaded blocks of cross-attention vision transformers. Cross-attention mechanism between latents and image features serve to enhance representational learning of local and global context. Meanwhile, latent and noise injections at each network layer permit fine control of generated image features, improving model invertibility. Demonstrations are performed for scan-specific reconstruction of brain MRI data at multiple contrasts and acceleration factors. GVTrans yields superior performance to state-of-the-art generative models based on convolutional neural networks (CNNs).

Keywords: MRI reconstruction · Transformer · Generative ·
Attention · Unsupervised

1 Introduction

Magnetic resonance imaging (MRI) is pervasive in non-invasive assessment of tissue morphology. However, its inherently slow acquisition process limits practical utility in many clinical applications, so there is emergent interest in accelerated MRI methods. Deep neural networks (DNN) have revolutionized accelerated MRI by offering state-of-the-art reconstruction performance

N. Haq et al. (Eds.): MLMIR 2021, LNCS 12964, pp. 54–64, 2021.
https://doi.org/10.1007/978-3-030-88552-6_6

from undersampled acquisitions. Supervised learning is the mainstream approach for training DNNs, where a large dataset is utilized containing fully-sampled acquisitions in conjunction with retrospectively undersampled counterparts [1,2,4,6,8,13,14,17,21,25,27,29]. Unfortunately, it is challenging to compile such large datasets for each imaging scenario. When ground truth data are scarce, complex network models can then suffer from non-convergent learning and poor generalization [5,9].

To alleviate data requirements for deep models, unsupervised learning frameworks have recently been introduced for MRI reconstruction. Prior unsupervised modeling approaches include transfer learning [5,9], cycle-consistent learning to permit use of unpaired training datasets [15,19,20], and self-supervised learning to completely remove dependency on fully-sampled ground truth data [16,22,24,26]. Yet, these previous methods still require large datasets to train models offline. A powerful alternative for unsupervised MRI reconstruction is based on the deep image prior (DIP) framework [18,23]. DIP performs inference on test data via randomly initialized convolutional neural network (CNN) models serving as native image regularizers [3,11]. Specifically, model inversion is performed to optimize the latent variables and network weights that maximize consistency of the network output to acquired k-space data. While DIP methods permit scan-specific reconstructions without a priori training, their performance is limited by the low sensitivity of CNNs to long-range dependencies that also compromises model invertibility [7].

In this study, we introduce an unsupervised MRI reconstruction based on a novel vision transformer (GVTrans) to improve representational learning of contextual features. The proposed architecture performs a nonlinear forward mapping from an input space containing noise and latent variables onto the MRI image. To enhance model invertibility, the nonlinear mapping is based on a style-generative architecture [12] that permits elevated control over generated feature maps. To improve sensitivity and disentanglement for global and local context, our architecture comprises novel cross-attention transformer blocks. These blocks learn long-range relationships between latents and image features without the computational burden of traditional transformers [10]. The proposed method does not require pre-training of network models or fully-sampled ground truth data. It adapts the network model to each test subject individually, offering enhanced generalization capabilities. Demonstrations are performed on accelerated brain MRI at multiple tissue contrasts and acceleration rates. Comparisons are provided against DIP-type reconstructions based on a fully-convolutional generative model [12], and a self-attention CNN-based generative model [28]. Our results clearly indicate that GVTrans has improved invertibility, contextual sensitivity and disentanglement between local and global features compared to state-of-the-art generative models based on CNNs.

2   Theory

2.1   Deep Unsupervised MRI Reconstruction

MRI acquisitions can be accelerated via undersampling in the Fourier domain
(i.e., k-space):

$$F_u Cm = y_s \tag{1}$$

where F_u is the partial Fourier operator defined on the set of sampled k-space
locations, C denotes sensitivity maps of coil elements, m is the underlying MR
image and y_s are collected k-space data. To reconstruct the image m given y_s,
the underdetermined system in Eq. 1 must be solved. To improve the conditioning of the problem, prior information on the MR image is incorporated as a
regularization term:

$$\widehat{m} = \underset{m}{\operatorname{argmin}} \|y_s - F_u Cm\|_2^2 + H(m) \tag{2}$$

where $\widehat{m}$ is the reconstruction, and $H(m)$ is the regularization. In deep learning
reconstructions, the regularization function that is typically implemented as a
projection through a CNN architecture that suppresses aliasing artifacts. In the
supervised learning setup, model training is performed on a large dataset of fully-
sampled ground truth MRI data. The CNN weights are learned to effectively map
undersampled MRI data onto high-quality MR images that resemble ground
truth data as closely as possible.

To mitigate reliance on fully-sampled ground truths, the deep image prior
(DIP) framework observes that CNNs performing filtering with local kernels can
serve as native image regularizers. As such, DIP-based reconstructions randomly
initialize the network inputs and weights. Without any training, inference is
performed directly on each given test subject starting with the untrained network
model. In the case of MRI, to ensure that the network output maintains fidelity
to the physical signal model, network inputs and weights are adapted to ensure
maximal consistency to the acquired k-space data [3,11]. This process is known
as model inversion, and the resulting reconstruction can then be formulated as:

$$\theta^* = \underset{\theta}{\operatorname{argmin}} \|F_u C d_\theta(z) - y_s\|_1 \tag{3}$$

where θ are network weights, z are latent variables, $d_\theta(z)$ is the projection from
latents onto the reconstruction. Network weights and latents are randomly initialized, and the optimization in Eq. 3 is performed over θ, while z is fixed. The
reconstructed image can be obtained as:

$$\widehat{m} = d_{\theta^*}(z) \tag{4}$$

2.2   Generative Vision Transformers

DIP-type MRI reconstruction eliminates the need to collect experimentally
costly ground truth acquisitions, and model pre-training on large databases.

That said, existing DIP methods for MRI are based on purely convolutional architectures. CNN-based models have limited sensitivity to long-range spatial dependencies among image features [10], and theoretical and empirical work suggest that they have sub-optimal invertibility [7]. To address these fundamental problems, here we propose a novel generative vision transformer (GVTrans) for unsupervised MRI reconstruction (Fig. 1). Based on the DIP framework, GVTrans performs a forward mapping from noise and latent variables onto MR images, and inverts this mapping to infer network parameters most consistent with the acquired data under the MR signal model. In contrast the prior approaches, GVTrans leverages a style-generative adversarial architecture with cross-attention transformer blocks between latents and image features.

Network Architecture. GVTrans is a style-generative network architecture inspired by the StyleGAN model [12] popular in computer vision tasks. Accordingly, it contains an unconditional synthesizer network that receives noise and latent inputs and progressively maps them onto MRI images across multiple layers of increasing spatial resolution. Uniquely in GVTrans, we propose to build the progressive network layers via cross-attention transformer blocks as opposed to CNN layers in StyleGAN (Fig. 1). These cross-attention transformer blocks received as input global and local latent variables to control capture of both global and local context at each layer ($w_g \in \mathbb{R}^L$ and $W_l \in \mathbb{R}^{k \times L}$). Vanilla transformer architectures with exhaustive self-attention have high computational burden that prohibit their use in high-resolution image processing tasks. Here we instead build the transformer encoders by interleaving layers of cross-attention modules and modulated convolutions. The cross-attention module controls produced feature maps via the latent variables. Let $X_{vec}^i \in \mathbb{R}^{(m \times h) \times v}$ be vectorized $X^i \in \mathbb{R}^{m \times h \times v}$ across spatial dimensions. Cross-attention maps $att_i \in \mathbb{R}^{(m \times h) \times v}$ between W_l and X_{vec}^i are computed as:

$$att_G^i = softmax\left(\frac{q_G^i(X_{vec}^i)k_G^i(W_l)^T}{\sqrt{v}}\right)v_G^i(W_l) \qquad (5)$$

where $q_G^i(.) \in \mathbb{R}^{(m \times h) \times v}$, $k_i(.) \in \mathbb{R}^{k \times v}$, and $v_G^i(.) \in \mathbb{R}^{k \times v}$ are queries, keys and values. The embeddings for queries, keys and values are supplemented with positional encoding variables. Next, X_{vec}^i is scaled and shifted with learnable projections of attention maps att_G^i:

$$X_{vec}'^i = \gamma_i(att_G^i) \odot \left(\frac{X_{vec}^i - \mu(X_{vec}^i)}{\sigma(X_{vec}^i)}\right) + b_i(att_G^i) \qquad (6)$$

where $\gamma_i(.)$ and $b_i(.)$ are learned projections. Attention-based contextual representations are then further processed with convolution modules as an efficient implementation of feed-forward neural network (FFNN) mapping in transformers. At the ith convolution module, input features are modulated with

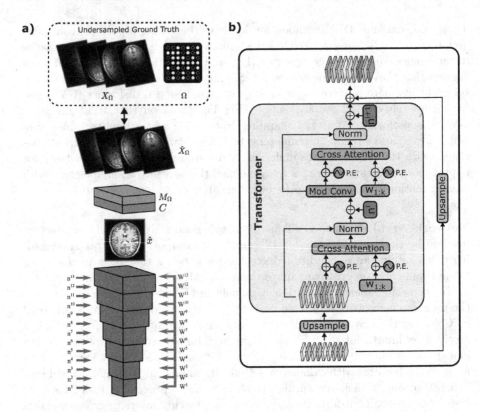

Fig. 1. GVTrans is a deep generative network that maps noise variables (n) and latents (W) onto high-quality MR images. The multi-layer architecture progressive increases image resolution. Within each layer, upsampled feature maps are input to a cross-attention transformer module (see the right panel). For inference on test data, the generated MR images are masked with the same sampling pattern as in the under-sampled acquisition. Network parameters are optimized to ensure consistency between reconstructed and original k-space samples.

affine-transformed global latent variables ($w_s^i \in \mathbb{R}^u$ derived from w_g). To do this, scaled convolution kernels θ_G^i are used to filter the feature maps:

$$X''^i = \begin{bmatrix} \sum_s X'^{i-1,s} \circledast \theta_G^{i,s,1} \\ \vdots \\ \sum_s X'^{i-1,s} \circledast \theta_G^{i,s,v} \end{bmatrix} + \begin{bmatrix} \alpha^{i,1} n^{i,1} \\ \vdots \\ \alpha^{i,v} n^{i,v} \end{bmatrix} \tag{7}$$

where $\theta_G^{i,u',v'} \in \mathbb{R}^{r \times r}$ is the convolution kernel for the $u'th$ input channel and $v'th$ output channel, and s is the channel index. Furthermore, noise variables are injected onto feature maps $n^{i,v'} \in \mathbb{R}^{m \times h}$ is spatially-varying noise on the $v'th$ channel of ith layer and $\alpha^{i,v}$ is a learnable scalar.

Unsupervised Reconstruction. The randomly initialized generative model is inverted to perform unsupervised MRI reconstruction. To do this, a selective loss function is defined in k-space to ensure consistency of Fourier-domain representations of reconstructed and acquired data:

$$L_m(W, n, \theta) = \|F_u G(W, n, \theta) - y_s\|_1 \tag{8}$$

where $\hat{m}$: reconstructed image, y_s: acquired k-space data, G: generative network, n: noise and θ_G: network weights. Inference is performed by optimizing noise, latents and weights to ensure data fidelity.

3 Methods

Datasets. We performed demonstrations on two public neuroimaging datasets: IXI (http://brain-development.org/) and fastMRI (https://fastmri.org/). In IXI, T_1- and T_2-weighted images of 40 subjects were analyzed (25 for training, 5 for validation, 10 for testing). In fastMRI, T_1- and T_2-weighted images from 150 subjects were analyzed (100 for training, 10 for validation, 40 for testing). Variable-density random sampling was used for retrospective undersampling. Sampling density was taken as a 2D normal distribution with covariance adjusted to achieve acceleration factors of R = 4, 8.

Baselines. GVTrans was compared against state-of-the-art generative models with CNN backbones. Hyperparameter selection for each competing method was performed via cross-validation. Inference procedures during DIP-style reconstructions were identical for all methods. Implementations were run on nVidia 2080 Ti GPUs using TensorFlow in Python.

GAN: A style-generative network model with CNN layers of progressively increasing resolution was considered. The network architecture for GAN was adopted from [12].

SAGAN: A self-attention generative model previously proposed for improved learning of long-range dependencies in CNNs was also considered. The network architecture for SAGAN was adopted from [12].

Experiments. DIP-type reconstructions were performed on undersampled acquisitions. Network models were randomly initialized with latents, noise and network weights drawn from a standard normal distribution. Network parameters were then optimized to maximize data consistency. Inference was performed with the RMSprop optimizer run for 1000 iterations and a learning schedule adopted from [12]. Following the final iteration, strict data consistency was enforced. In fastMRI, reconstructions were mapped onto single coils to define the selective loss in Eq. 8 per coil.

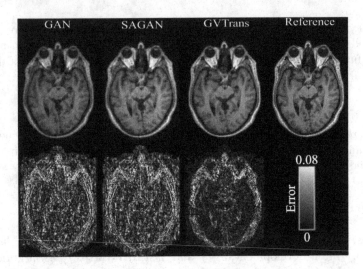

Fig. 2. Representative T_1-weighted MRI reconstructions and respective error maps in IXI at R = 4. Results are shown along with the reference image.

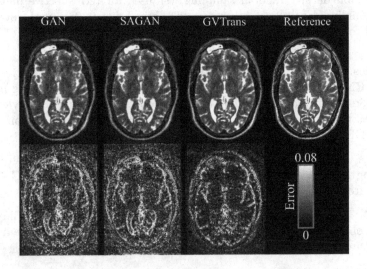

Fig. 3. Representative T_2-weighted MRI reconstructions and respective error maps in IXI at R = 4. Results are shown for along with the reference image.

Performance Evaluation. Reconstruction quality was evaluated by measuring peak signal-to-noise ratio (PSNR) and structural similarity index (SSIM) between the reconstructed and reference fully-sampled MR images. In Tables, metrics are reported as mean ± std across test subjects. Statistical differences between reconstruction methods were assessed via Wilcoxon signed-rank tests.

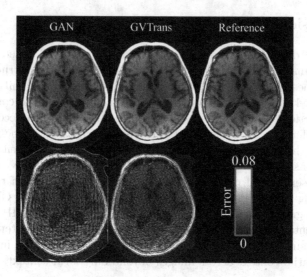

Fig. 4. Representative T_1-weighted MRI reconstructions and respective error maps in fastMRI at R = 4. Results are shown along with the reference image. SAGAN was excluded in this case as it yields on par results with GAN.

Table 1. Reconstruction performance for T_1- and T_2-weighted images in the IXI dataset at R = 4 and 8.

	GAN		SAGAN		GVTrans	
	PSNR	SSIM(%)	PSNR	SSIM(%)	PSNR	SSIM(%)
T_1, R = 4	26.67 ± 1.22	87.37 ± 0.99	26.60 ± 1.10	86.48 ± 0.99	$\mathbf{32.55 \pm 1.77}$	$\mathbf{94.58 \pm 0.82}$
T_1, R = 8	23.45 ± 0.92	83.02 ± 1.13	23.42 ± 0.90	82.50 ± 1.17	$\mathbf{30.28 \pm 1.68}$	$\mathbf{91.64 \pm 1.42}$
T_2, R = 4	30.23 ± 0.45	80.77 ± 1.22	29.90 ± 0.40	79.41 ± 1.36	$\mathbf{32.71 \pm 0.73}$	$\mathbf{87.66 \pm 1.67}$
T_2, R = 8	27.64 ± 0.38	76.16 ± 1.30	27.28 ± 0.37	74.06 ± 1.57	$\mathbf{29.90 \pm 0.70}$	$\mathbf{84.03 \pm 1.89}$

4   Results

We compared GVTrans against state-of-the-art generative models based on CNN backbones. Baselines included a progressive style-generative architecture (GAN) and self-attention modulated generative architecture (SAGAN). Representative reconstructions of T_1- and T_2-weighted images in IXI are displayed in Figs. 2 and 3, and representative results for T_1-weighted images in fastMRI are displayed in Fig. 4. Quantitative performance metrics over the test set are listed for IXI in Table 1. GVTrans yields superior performance against GAN and SAGAN both visually and quantitatively for all contrasts and acceleration factors ($p < 0.05$). Compared to the second-best method, GVTrans yields 4.36dB higher PSNR and 7.65% higher SSIM. These results indicate that the cross-attention transformer blocks in GVTrans enhance model invertibility compared to CNN-based generative architectures with or without self-attention mechanisms.

5 Discussion

Here, we introduced an unsupervised reconstruction model based on generative vision transformers. GVTrans can perform DIP-type reconstructions, so it bypasses the need for a priori model training. Instead, randomly initialized models are inverted to optimize network parameters that maximize consistency of the reconstruction to the acquired k-space data. While DIP-type reconstructions have longer inference times compared to reconstructions with offline-trained network models, the scan-specific nature of GVTrans can improve generalizability. Furthermore, as opposed to classical models backboned with CNN architectures that only preserve local dependencies, GVTrans leverages vision transformers to capture long-range dependencies. In the reported experiments, GVTrans was observed to significantly improve image quality compared to DIP reconstructions implemented via CNN-based models with and without self-attention blocks. These results suggest that MRI reconstructions can benefits from incorporation of broader spatial context across images beyond only local context.

6 Conclusion

In this study, we introduced a novel unsupervised MRI reconstruction approach by embedding vision transformers into a generative network, and performing scan-specific reconstructions as inspired by the deep image prior framework. GVTrans offers improved image quality compared to CNN-based reconstructions with and without self-attention mechanisms, and it can flexibly adapt its model to individual test subjects. Therefore, GVTrans is a promising candidate for improving the applicability and generalizability of deep MRI reconstructions.

References

1. Adler, J., Öktem, O.: Learned primal-dual reconstruction. IEEE Trans. Med. Imaging **37**(6), 1322–1332 (2018)
2. Aggarwal, H.K., Mani, M.P., Jacob, M.: MoDL: model-based deep learning architecture for inverse problems. IEEE Trans. Med. Imaging **38**(2), 394–405 (2019)
3. Biswas, S., Aggarwal, H.K., Jacob, M.: Dynamic MRI using model-based deep learning and SToRM priors: MoDL-SToRM. Magn. Reson. Med. **82**(1), 485–494 (2019)
4. Dar, S.U.H., Yurt, M., Shahdloo, M., Ildız, M.E., Tınaz, B., Çukur, T.: Prior-guided image reconstruction for accelerated multi-contrast MRI via generative adversarial networks. IEEE J. Sel. Top. Sig. Process. **14**(6), 1072–1087 (2020)
5. Dar, S.U.H., Özbey, M., Çatlı, A.B., Çukur, T.: A transfer-learning approach for accelerated MRI using deep neural networks. Magn. Reson. Med. **84**(2), 663–685 (2020)
6. Eo, T., Jun, Y., Kim, T., Jang, J., Lee, H.J., Hwang, D.: KIKI-net: cross-domain convolutional neural networks for reconstructing undersampled magnetic resonance images. Magn. Reson. Med. **80**(5), 2188–2201 (2018)
7. Gabbay, A., Hoshen, Y.: Style generator inversion for image enhancement and animation. arXiv preprint arXiv:1906.11880 (2019)

8. Hammernik, K., et al.: Learning a variational network for reconstruction of accelerated MRI data. Magn. Reson. Med. **79**(6), 3055–3071 (2017)
9. Han, Y., Yoo, J., Kim, H.H., Shin, H.J., Sung, K., Ye, J.C.: Deep learning with domain adaptation for accelerated projection-reconstruction MR. Magn. Reson. Med. **80**(3), 1189–1205 (2018). https://doi.org/10.1002/mrm.27106
10. Hudson, D.A., Zitnick, C.L.: Generative adversarial transformers. arXiv preprint arXiv:2103.01209 (2021)
11. Jin, K.H., Gupta, H., Yerly, J., Stuber, M., Unser, M.: Time-dependent deep image prior for dynamic MRI. arXiv preprint arXiv:1910.01684 (2019)
12. Karras, T., Laine, S., Aittala, M., Hellsten, J., Lehtinen, J., Aila, T.: Analyzing and improving the image quality of StyleGAN. In: Proceedings of the IEEE/CVF Conference on Computer Vision and Pattern Recognition (CVPR), pp. 8107–8116 (2020)
13. Kwon, K., Kim, D., Park, H.: A parallel MR imaging method using multilayer perceptron. Med. Phys. **44**(12), 6209–6224 (2017). https://doi.org/10.1002/mp.12600
14. Lee, D., Yoo, J., Tak, S., Ye, J.C.: Deep residual learning for accelerated MRI using magnitude and phase networks. IEEE Trans. Biomed. Eng. **65**(9), 1985–1995 (2018)
15. Lei, K., Mardani, M., Pauly, J.M., Vasanawala, S.S.: Wasserstein GANs for MR imaging: from paired to unpaired training. IEEE Trans. Med. Imaging **40**(1), 105–115 (2021)
16. Liu, J., Sun, Y., Eldeniz, C., Gan, W., An, H., Kamilov, U.S.: RARE: image reconstruction using deep priors learned without groundtruth. IEEE J. Sel. Top. Sig. Process. **14**(6), 1088–1099 (2020)
17. Mardani, M., et al.: Deep generative adversarial neural networks for compressive sensing MRI. IEEE Trans. Med. Imaging **38**(1), 167–179 (2019)
18. Narnhofer, D., Hammernik, K., Knoll, F., Pock, T.: Inverse GANs for accelerated MRI reconstruction. In: Proceedings of the SPIE, vol. 11138, pp. 381–392 (2019)
19. Oh, G., Sim, B., Chung, H., Sunwoo, L., Ye, J.C.: Unpaired deep learning for accelerated MRI using optimal transport driven CycleGAN. IEEE Trans. Comput. Imaging **6**, 1285–1296 (2020)
20. Quan, T.M., Nguyen-Duc, T., Jeong, W.K.: Compressed sensing MRI reconstruction with cyclic loss in generative adversarial networks. IEEE Trans. Med. Imaging **37**(6), 1488–1497 (2018)
21. Schlemper, J., Caballero, J., Hajnal, J.V., Price, A., Rueckert, D.: A deep cascade of convolutional neural networks for MR image reconstruction. In: Niethammer, M., et al. (eds.) IPMI 2017. LNCS, vol. 10265, pp. 647–658. Springer, Cham (2017). https://doi.org/10.1007/978-3-319-59050-9_51
22. Tamir, J.I., Yu, S.X., Lustig, M.: Unsupervised deep basis pursuit: learning reconstruction without ground-truth data. In: Proceedings of the 27th Annual Meeting of the ISMRM, p. 0660 (2019)
23. Tezcan, K.C., Baumgartner, C.F., Luechinger, R., Pruessmann, K.P., Konukoglu, E.: MR image reconstruction using deep density priors. IEEE Trans. Med. Imaging **38**(7), 1633–1642 (2019)
24. Wang, A.Q., Dalca, A.V., Sabuncu, M.R.: Neural network-based reconstruction in compressed sensing MRI without fully-sampled training data. In: Deeba, F., Johnson, P., Würfl, T., Ye, J.C. (eds.) MLMIR 2020. LNCS, vol. 12450, pp. 27–37. Springer, Cham (2020). https://doi.org/10.1007/978-3-030-61598-7_3

25. Wang, S., et al.: Accelerating magnetic resonance imaging via deep learning. In: IEEE 13th International Symposium on Biomedical Imaging (ISBI), pp. 514–517 (2016). https://doi.org/10.1109/ISBI.2016.7493320
26. Yaman, B., Hosseini, S.A.H., Moeller, S., Ellermann, J., Uğurbil, K., Akçakaya, M.: Self-supervised learning of physics-guided reconstruction neural networks without fully sampled reference data. Magn. Reson. Med. **84**(6), 3172–3191 (2020)
27. Yu, S., et al.: DAGAN: deep de-aliasing generative adversarial networks for fast compressed sensing MRI reconstruction. IEEE Trans. Med. Imaging **37**(6), 1310–1321 (2018)
28. Zhang, H., Goodfellow, I., Metaxas, D., Odena, A.: Self-attention generative adversarial networks. In: Proceedings of the 36th International Conference on Machine Learning, pp. 7354–7363 (2019)
29. Zhu, B., Liu, J.Z., Rosen, B.R., Rosen, M.S.: Image reconstruction by domain transform manifold learning. Nature **555**(7697), 487–492 (2018)

Distortion Removal and Deblurring of Single-Shot DWI MRI Scans

Ahana Roy Choudhury[1]([✉]), Sachin R. Jambawalikar[2], Piyush Kumar[3], and Venkat Sumanth Reddy Bommireddy[3]

[1] Department of Computer Science, Valdosta State University, Valdosta, GA, USA
aroychoudhury@valdosta.edu
[2] Department of Radiology, Columbia University Medical Center, New York, USA
sj2532@cumc.columbia.edu
[3] Department of Computer Science, Florida State University, Tallahassee, FL, USA
piyush@cs.fsu.edu, vb19h@my.fsu.edu

Abstract. Diffusion Weighted Imaging (DWI) is one of the standard MRI images that are used for the diagnosis of brain tumors. However, the acquired DW images suffer from artifacts such as EPI (echo-planar imaging) distortion. These distortions are corrected using blip-up and blip-down images that are separately acquired for distortion removal. In addition, DWI MRI images have shorter acquisition times, but suffer from poor resolution. Multi-shot diffusion weighted imaging allows the acquisition of higher resolution images but require longer acquisition times and necessitate the use of new and expensive hardware. In this paper, we perform distortion removal of EPI-DWI images from blip-up images using a previously proposed framework and design a suitable deblurring technique for generating higher resolution DWI images from low-resolution undistorted EPI-DWI images. Our technique aims to allow the use of deblurred EPI-DWI images for performing accurate medical diagnosis and multi parametric longitudinal analysis in brain tumors. We use data augmentation, dilated convolution, and ELU (exponential linear unit) to design a suitable architecture that achieves superior performance in terms of accuracy.

Keywords: DWI · MRI · EPI-DWI · Multi-shot DWI · Convolutional neural network · Distortion removal · Super-resolution · Deblurring

1 Introduction

Diffusion Weighted Imaging (DWI) plays an important role in measuring the cellularity of tumors and can be used to detect the peritumoral edema region of a brain tumor. DWI images have been used to detect strokes, and the restricted diffusion in stroke is clearly visible in apparent diffusion coefficient (ADC) images derived from DWI. The identification of the edema region from the tumor core region plays an important role in brain tumor diagnosis. The hyper-intensity of the peritumoral edema and that of the tumor core can be distinguished using

© Springer Nature Switzerland AG 2021
N. Haq et al. (Eds.): MLMIR 2021, LNCS 12964, pp. 65–75, 2021.
https://doi.org/10.1007/978-3-030-88552-6_7

DWI images. Thus, DWI is one of the standard MR imaging techniques used for the diagnosis of brain tumors [22] and is essential for deciding the treatment that is provided to patients.

On the other hand, DWI is limited by magnetic resonance hardware. Firstly, for both single-shot and multi-shot DWI, blip-up and blip-down images need to be captured in order to perform distortion correction. This results in duplication of effort since two sets of DWI scans need to be acquired instead of one. Besides, single-shot echo-planar (EPI) DWI MRI images have shorter acquisition times of 30 to 40 s [20], but suffer from poor resolution, low signal-to-noise ratio, and are unsuitable for medical diagnosis [18]. However, EPI-DWI can be acquired using older hardware, and due to their shorter acquisition times, these images are less affected by distortion due to motion. In contrast, multi-shot DWI images, which have higher resolution and less image distortion, have longer acquisition times of 2 to 3 min and require the use of new and expensive hardware. While respiratory triggered DWI can be used for abdomen protocols, in clinical practice, respiratory triggering takes much longer as patient breathing is inconsistent throughout the scan and shallow breathing does not trigger the scan acquisition. In body MR protocols free breathing low resolution DWI scans are mostly preferred instead of respiratory triggering as a high percentage of respiratory triggered scans fail and need to be repeated. So, for high-resolution DW images, the state-of-the-art technique involves the use of multi-shot DW images. However, the longer acquisition times for multi-shot DWI mean that the acquisition of multi-shot DWI images requires the patient to remain still and hold their breath for a longer period of time. In cases where the patient fails to do so, the acquired image is distorted and suffers from motion artifacts. Besides, the cost of upgrading to newer machines, that are used for acquiring the multi-shot DW images, ranges from $250k to $1 million [9]. While scanner hardware and software decisions are not based on a single acquisition protocol, using deep learning to generate super-resolved images from EPI-DWI images can make it possible to get comparable image quality (without scanner upgrade) to current state of the art acquisition techniques (high resolution distortion free scans) for DW imaging. Such deep learning techniques can be utilized on the existing scanner platform without any hardware or pulse sequence upgrade.

Since the multi-shot DWI images suffer from the drawbacks of having a longer acquisition time as well as requiring the use of more expensive hardware, and the major shortcoming of EPI-DWI is its low resolution; an automatic system for the generation of higher resolution images from EPI-DWI images will resolve the issues of longer acquisition times and expensive hardware while ensuring higher resolution and suitability for medical diagnosis. Besides, our framework performs automatic distortion removal using blip-up images and structural images only and does not require the use of blip-down images. Thus, it additionally reduces the amount of manual labor and intervention involved in the process of acquiring MRI images.

While traditional techniques including bilinear, nearest neighbor and bicubic interpolation can be used to perform super-resolution of images, they result in blurry images that lack details. CNN-based super-resolution techniques are known to improve the accuracy of super-resolved images [6, 7, 14, 15, 24–26] because deep neural networks can learn complex functions and have been shown to generate images that closely resemble high-resolution images. Generative Adversarial Networks (GANs), achieve improved performance for the task of super-resolution [13, 24, 26]. However, other techniques that involve the use of a single CNN show comparable or superior performance if the architecture and the loss function are designed appropriately [2, 10, 14, 15, 25]. A significant amount of work has been done in the field of architectural design for super-resolution including the exploration of different loss functions [2, 10].

In medical imaging, super-resolution and deblurring of medical images using deep learning [1, 11, 12, 16, 17, 21] has received some attention too. Zeng et al. [12] simultaneously perform single and multi-contrast MRI super-resolution. In [4], Chen et al. introduce 3D Densely Connected Super-Resolution Networks (DCSRN), to perform super-resolution of structural brain MR images. Gholizadeh-Ansari et al. [8] propose the use of dilated convolutions with different dilation rates and shortcut connections to denoise low-dose CT. In [11], the authors attempt to improve the resolution of the Whole-heart coronary magnetic resonance angiography (WHCMRA) using a CNN. Besides, several attempts have been made to use GANs [1, 16, 17, 23] for super-resolution or image-to-image translation of medical images involving, but not limited to, the use of different loss functions [16, 17]. However, super-resolution or deblurring of EPI-DWI images to generate higher resolution multi-shot DWI images has not attracted much attention.

In this paper, we design a deep learning based framework that generates undistorted, high resolution DWI images from distorted blip-up EPI-DWI images. The proposed framework reduces the amount of human intervention by performing distortion removal using blip-up images. Besides, it ensures that we can generate images that are suitable for medical diagnosis by using the older and cheaper hardware that is utilized for acquiring EPI-DWI images. Specifically, our system is broken up into two parts, where the first one uses an existing technique to utilize the MP-RAGE T1 MRI scans for generating the undistorted EPI-DWI images from the distorted EPI blip-up images. Secondly, we modify a CNN architecture that performs super-resolution. Using the distortion removed EPI-DWI images as the low-resolution, blurred images, we train a CNN architecture by using the multi-shot DWI images as the deblurred, high-resolution images. We use the EDSR architecture [14] and modify it to perform deblurring and to achieve superior performance. We tackle this problem in 2D and experimentally identify the architecture that achieves the best performance in terms of the accuracy of the deblurred images.

2 Background

2.1 Distortion Removal Framework

For distortion removal, we utilize the technique proposed in [19]. The inputs to the network are the structural image and the distorted b0 image. The network is a modified version of 3D U-Net, which uses LeakyReLU and instance normalization. The training is performed for 100 epochs using Adam optimizer and the loss used is mean-squared-error (MSE). Five-fold cross-validation is used in the paper and the resultant undistorted image is generated by using an ensemble of the five models trained in this process. For postprocessing, some smoothing is applied to the distorted b0 image in order to make it compatible to the undistorted b0 image. Finally, the distorted and the undistorted b0 images are used as the inputs to the topup software and the resultant parameters are saved.

2.2 EDSR Architecture

In our work, we use the EDSR architecture [14], which was the winner of the 2017 NITRE challenge. Since then, this architecture has been used as a baseline for a significant amount of research work in the field of super-resolution of images. Thus, we select this network as our baseline and experiment with various modifications of this model.

The EDSR architecture uses residual blocks due to the ease of training residual networks. EDSR makes modifications to the ResNet block used in the SRResNet architecture [13] by removing the batch normalization layers. This layer is not useful for the task of super-resolution since it normalizes the features and removes the range flexibility of the model. The removal of the batch normalization layers significantly reduces the GPU memory usage, and this allows the use of a deeper CNN with a larger number of feature channels. Specifically, the EDSR architecture consists of a first convolutional layer that uses a 3×3 kernel to convolve on the input image and produce a 256 channel feature map as the output. Next, it contains $n = 32$ residual blocks, where the last block is followed by another convolution. The next block, the Upsampler, consists of PixelShuffle[1] and convolutional layers to perform upsampling. The final convolution converts the 256 channel feature map to an output image consisting of the expected number of channels. The loss used for training is L1 loss.

3 Distortion Removal and Deblurring of EPI-DWI

3.1 Data

The data that we use for our experiments consists of 10 samples of MRI brain data acquired from patients. The data is acquired as DICOM images, and we convert that into NIFTI images in order to perform our experiments. Specifically, the image types that we use for our experiments are as follows:

---

[1] https://pytorch.org/docs/stable/generated/torch.nn.PixelShuffle.html.

- **T1 MP-RAGE Structural Image:** The structural image is used for distortion removal. This image is acquired sagittally and has a reconstruction matrix size of $512 \times 512 \times 292$
- **Forward EPI-DWI (blip-up) image:** This image consists of 5 volumes. Of these, we use the b0 image (volume 2) for distortion removal and both distortion removal and deblurring are performed on the DWI image (volume 1). This image is acquired axially, has a reconstruction matrix size of $256 \times 256 \times 32$ with an acquisition matrix of size 120×120. The voxel size is $2\,\mathrm{mm} \times 2\,\mathrm{mm} \times 4\,\mathrm{mm}$.
- **Multi-shot (MUSE) DWI Image:** This is the high-resolution image. This image is acquired axially, and the size is $256 \times 256 \times 32$ with an acquisition matrix of 224×224. The voxel size is $1.07\,\mathrm{mm} \times 1.07\,\mathrm{mm} \times 4\,\mathrm{mm}$.

3.2 Distortion Removal Using Structural Images

For distortion removal, we utilize the technique proposed in [19]. We use the pre-trained models and the docker provided by the authors. The distortion removal is performed initially on the b0 image, and this gives us the necessary parameters for performing the distortion removal of the DWI images. For each b0 image, we save the corresponding parameters from the topup software[2] and then utilize these parameters to apply topup for distortion removal of the DWI images.

3.3 Pre-processing for Super-Resolution

For the purpose of our deblurring experiments, we register the distortion removed EPI-DWI images to the multi-shot DWI images by using ANTs[3]. We then divide our dataset into three splits: train, validation, and test. Our training set consists of 6 of the 10 cases, while the validation and test sets consist of 2 cases each. Then, we perform slicing in order to obtain 32 axial slices from each of our 10 3D EPI-DWI and multi-shot DWI images.

3.4 Data Augmentation

Since the size of our data set is quite small, we introduce data augmentation to improve the quality of our results. The augmentations are used only during training in order to improve the generalization capability of the trained model. The augmentations used are:

- Rotate: Rotate randomly by $0°$, $90°$, $180°$, or $270°$
- Transpose: Matrix transpose is applied to the image with a probability of 50%.
- Horizontal Flip: This is applied to the image with a probability of 50%.
- Vertical Flip: This is applied to the image with a probability of 50%.

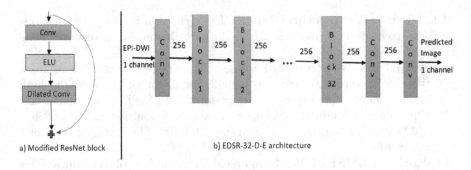

Fig. 1. Diagrammatic representation of the EDSR-32-D-E architecture, which is our proposed architecture. **a)** Modified ResNet block that uses dilated convolution and ELU **b)** Shows a representation of EDSR-32 architecture.

3.5 Architectures Explored for EPI-DWI Deblurring

In this sub-section, we discuss the details of the architectures that we explore for performing deblurring of EPI-DWI images.

- **EDSR with 32 ResNet Blocks (EDSR-32):** This is the original EDSR architecture presented in [14] and is described in detail in Sect. 2.2. Since our low and high resolution images have the same number of pixels and the variation lies in the size of the acquisition matrices only, we remove the use of the Upsampling module.
- **EDSR with 8 ResNet Blocks (EDSR-8):** This model consists of 8 ResNet blocks, and all other parts of the architecture are the same as the EDSR-32 architecture.
- **EDSR with 32 ResNet Blocks and dilated convolution (EDSR-32-D):** This model consists of the 32 block EDSR model, EDSR-32, but uses dilated convolution with a dilation of 2 for the second convolution in each block. The concept of using dilated convolutions in computer vision was popularized in [3].
- **EDSR with 32 ResNet Blocks, dilated convolution, and ELU (EDSR-32-D-E):** This model consists of the 32 block EDSR model with dilated convolution, EDSR-32-D, but uses ELU [5] as the activation function instead of ReLU. As mentioned in [5], ELU is expected to improve the accuracy achieved by the model, since it introduces non-linearity but, unlike ReLU, does not give an output of zero for all values less than or equal to zero.

4 Experiments and Results

4.1 Computer Hardware Details

Our experiments are performed on an Intel Core i7 CPU with a Nvidia GeForce GTX 1080 Ti GPU that has 11 GB memory.

---

[2] https://fsl.fmrib.ox.ac.uk/fsl/fslwiki/topup.
[3] http://stnava.github.io/ANTs/.

4.2 Training Details

Our training data consists of 192 high-resolution and low-resolution image pairs. We extract 16 patches of size 64×64 from each slice. Thus, our training set consists of 3072 patches and our validation set consists of 64 slices, which are divided into 1024 patches.

For training the EDSR-8 architecture, a batch size of 16 is used. For the EDSR-32 architectures, we use a batch size of 8. A learning rate of 0.0001 is used and each model is trained for 300 epochs. The loss used for the EDSR models is L1 loss. For each architecture, we save the model corresponding to the epoch at which the best performance is obtained on the validation set and use it for inference on the test set.

4.3 Baselines

We use two baselines to compare our results in the results section:

- **Low-resolution images:** The input low-resolution, blurry images.
- **SRResNet:** We utilize the generator architecture proposed in [13] in order to perform the deblurring.

4.4 Evaluation Metrics

We use three metrics to evaluate and compare the performance of our models. The metrics used are:

- L1 loss
- Peak signal to noise ratio (PSNR)
- Structural similarity index measure (SSIM)

4.5 Results

In Table 1, we tabulate the results of the baseline techniques as well as the EDSR models. From the results, we see that the quality of deblurred images improves with the increase in the number of ResNet blocks used in the EDSR model. Besides, we compare to the low-resolution image to get a measure of the quality of the input image, which uses interpolation. We see that the result from EDSR-8 is better than SRResNet even though SRResNet has 16 ResNet blocks. This is due to the larger number of feature channels used in EDSR in comparison to SRResNet, which has 64.

The introduction of data augmentation results in an improvement in the accuracy too because of the small size of the training set. In Table 1, we compare the performance of the EDSR-32 model with and without augmentation to measure the improvement due to data augmentation.

Besides using the EDSR models of varying depths, we experiment with EDSR architectures consisting of 32 blocks by utilizing dilated convolution in each block

(EDSR-32-D). In Table 1, we compare the results of models EDSR-32, EDSR-32-D and EDSR-32-D-E, where EDSR-32-D-E uses ELU as the activation function instead of ReLU. We see that the results improve progressively from EDSR-32 to EDSR-32-D and finally, EDSR-32-D-E gives the best results.

Table 1. Comparison of accuracy of state-of-the-art methods and our architectures

Architecture	Augmentation	L1 Loss	PSNR (dB)	SSIM
LR	-	57.260	31.1759	0.8669
SRResNet	No	43.858	32.8724	0.9047
EDSR-8	No	37.245	34.0145	0.9145
EDSR-32	No	37.097	34.0894	0.9175
EDSR-32	Yes	35.816	34.2810	0.9170
EDSR-32-D	Yes	35.339	34.3986	**0.9183**
EDSR-32-D-E	Yes	**34.909**	**34.5086**	**0.9183**

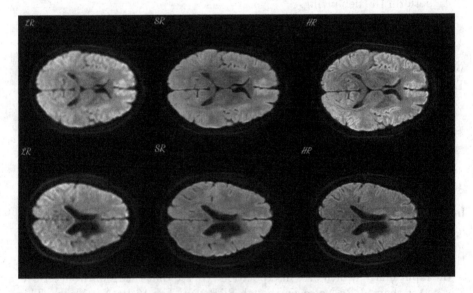

Fig. 2. Visual comparison of the low-resolution, super-resolution and high-resolution images. Left to right: LR, deblurred, and HR.

In Fig. 2, we provide the low-resolution, deblurred and high-resolution images. The deblurred images depicted in the figure are generated using the EDSR-32-D-E model.

5   Conclusion

This paper uses distorted EPI-DWI images and structural T1 MP-RAGE MRI scans to perform distortion removal. This eliminates the need of capturing the blip-down images and allows distortion removal to be performed using only the blip-up images. Then, we use undistorted EPI-DWI images to generate deblurred images similar to multi-shot DWI images. Since EPI-DWI images have shorter acquisition times, they are not as severely affected by motion artifacts. However, they have lower resolution and are harder to use for medical diagnosis and longitudinal analysis. Multi-shot DWI images have higher resolution, but have longer acquisition times, suffer from motion artifacts and require expensive hardware. Our framework enables the use of cheaper hardware and smaller acquisition times to generate higher resolution, deblurred DWI images that are suitable for medical diagnosis. We experiment with various architectures utilizing data augmentation, dilated convolutions, and ELU activation for deblurring and identify an architecture that achieves superior performance in terms of the quality of the generated images.

In future, we want to explore the use of perceptual loss for training and utilize Mean Opinion Score from radiologists to evaluate and compare the models.

References

1. Armanious, K., et al.: MedGAN: Medical image translation using GANs. CoRR abs/1806.06397 (2018). http://arxiv.org/abs/1806.06397
2. Bruna, J., Sprechmann, P., LeCun, Y.: Super-resolution with deep convolutional sufficient statistics. CoRR abs/1511.05666v4 (2016). https://arxiv.org/abs/1511.05666v4
3. Chen, L.C., Papandreou, G., Kokkinos, I., Murphy, K., Yuille, A.L.: DeepLab: Semantic image segmentation with deep convolutional nets, atrous convolution, and fully connected CRFs. IEEE Trans. Pattern Anal. Mach. Intell. **40**(4), 834–848 (2018)
4. Chen, Y., Xie, Y., Zhou, Z., Shi, F., Christodoulou, A., Li, D.: Brain MRI super resolution using 3d deep densely connected neural networks. In: Proceedings/IEEE International Symposium on Biomedical Imaging: from nano to macro, pp. 739–742 (2018). https://doi.org/10.1109/ISBI.2018.8363679
5. Clevert, D.A., Unterthiner, T., Hochreiter, S.: Fast and accurate deep network learning by exponential linear units (ELUS). CoRR abs/1511.07289 (2016). https://arxiv.org/abs/1511.07289
6. Dong, C., Loy, C.C., He, K., Tang, X.: Image super-resolution using deep convolutional networks. IEEE Trans. Pattern Anal. Mach. Intell. **38**, 295–307 (2016)
7. Dong, C., Loy, C.C., He, K., Tang, X.: Learning a deep convolutional network for image super-resolution. In: Fleet, D., Pajdla, T., Schiele, B., Tuytelaars, T. (eds.) ECCV 2014. LNCS, vol. 8692, pp. 184–199. Springer, Cham (2014). https://doi.org/10.1007/978-3-319-10593-2_13
8. Gholizadeh-Ansari, M., Alirezaie, J., Babyn, P.: Deep learning for low-dose CT denoising using perceptual loss and edge detection layer. J. Digit. Imag. **33**, 504–515 (2020). https://doi.org/10.1007/s10278-019-00274-4

9. Holtrop, J.L., Sutton, B.P.: High spatial resolution diffusion weighted imaging on clinical 3 T MRI scanners using multislab spiral acquisitions. J. Med. Imag. (Bellingham, Wash.) **3**, 023501 (2016). https://doi.org/10.1117/1.JMI.3.2.023501

10. Johnson, J., Alahi, A., Fei-Fei, L.: Perceptual losses for real-time style transfer and super-resolution. In: Leibe, B., Matas, J., Sebe, N., Welling, M. (eds.) ECCV 2016. LNCS, vol. 9906, pp. 694–711. Springer, Cham (2016). https://doi.org/10.1007/978-3-319-46475-6_43

11. Kobayashi, H., Nakayama, R., Hizukuri, A., Ishida, M., Kitagawa, K., Sakuma, H.: Improving image resolution of whole-heart coronary MRA using convolutional neural network. J. Digit. Imag. **33**, 497–503 (2019). https://doi.org/10.1007/s10278-019-00264-6

12. Kun, Z., Zheng, H., Cai, C., Yang, Y., Zhang, K., Chen, Z.: Simultaneous single- and multi-contrast super-resolution for brain MRI images based on a convolutional neural network. Comput. Biol. Med. **99**, 133–141 (2018). https://doi.org/10.1016/j.compbiomed.2018.06.010

13. Ledig, C., et al.: Photo-realistic single image super-resolution using a generative adversarial network. CoRR abs/1609.04802 (2016). http://arxiv.org/abs/1609.04802

14. Lim, B., Son, S., Kim, H., Nah, S., Lee, K.M.: Enhanced deep residual networks for single image super-resolution. CoRR abs/1707.02921 (2017). http://arxiv.org/abs/1707.02921

15. Liu, J., Zhang, W., Tang, Y., Tang, J., Wu, G.: Residual feature aggregation network for image super-resolution. In: Proceedings of the IEEE/CVF Conference on Computer Vision and Pattern Recognition (CVPR), June 2020

16. Mahapatra, D., Bozorgtabar, B.: Progressive generative adversarial networks for medical image super resolution. CoRR abs/1902.02144 (2019). http://arxiv.org/abs/1902.02144

17. Nie, D., et al.: Medical image synthesis with deep convolutional adversarial networks. IEEE Trans. Biomed. Eng. **65**(12), 2720–2730 (2018). https://doi.org/10.1109/TBME.2018.2814538

18. Scherrer, B., Afacan, O., Taquet, M., Prabhu, S.P., Gholipour, A., Warfield, S.K.: Accelerated high spatial resolution diffusion-weighted imaging. Inf. Process. Med. Imag. **24**, 69–81 (2015). https://doi.org/10.1007/978-3-319-19992-4_6

19. Schilling, K., et al.: Synthesized b0 for diffusion distortion correction (synb0-disco). Magn. Resonan. Imag. **64**, 62–70 (2019)

20. Skare, S., Newbould, R., Clayton, D., Albers, G., Nagle, S., Bammer, R.: Clinical multishot DW-EPI through parallel imaging with considerations of susceptibility, motion, and noise. Magn. Resonan. Med. Official J. Soc. Magn. Resonan. Med. Soc. Magn. Resonan. Med. **57**, 881–890 (2007). https://doi.org/10.1002/mrm.21176

21. Tan, C., Zhu, J., Lio', P.: Arbitrary scale super-resolution for brain MRI images. In: Maglogiannis, I., Iliadis, L., Pimenidis, E. (eds.) AIAI 2020. IAICT, vol. 583, pp. 165–176. Springer, Cham (2020). https://doi.org/10.1007/978-3-030-49161-1_15

22. Villanueva-Meyer, J.E., Mabray, M.C., Cha, S.: Current clinical brain tumor imaging. Neurosurgery **81**(3), 397–415 (2017). https://doi.org/10.1093/neuros/nyx103

23. Wang, J., Chen, Y., Wu, Y., Shi, J., Gee, J.: Enhanced generative adversarial network for 3D brain mri super-resolution. In: 2020 IEEE Winter Conference on Applications of Computer Vision (WACV), pp. 3616–3625 (2020). https://doi.org/10.1109/WACV45572.2020.9093603

24. Wang, X., et al.: ESRGAN: enhanced super-resolution generative adversarial networks. CoRR abs/1809.00219 (2018). http://arxiv.org/abs/1809.00219

25. Zhang, Y., Li, K., Li, K., Wang, L., Zhong, B., Fu, Y.: Image Super-Resolution Using Very Deep Residual Channel Attention Networks. In: 15th European Conference on Computer Vision, Munich, Germany, 8–14 September 2018, Proceedings, Part VII, pp. 294–310 (2018). https://doi.org/10.1007/978-3-030-01234-2_18

26. Zhu, J.Y., Park, T., Isola, P., Efros, A.: Unpaired image-to-image translation using cycle-consistent adversarial networks. In: 2017 IEEE International Conference on Computer Vision (ICCV), pp. 2242–2251 (2017)

One Network to Solve Them All: A Sequential Multi-task Joint Learning Network Framework for MR Imaging Pipeline

Zhiwen Wang[1], Wenjun Xia[1], Zexin Lu[1], Yongqiang Huang[1], Yan Liu[2], Hu Chen[1], Jiliu Zhou[3], and Yi Zhang[1(✉)]

[1] College of Computer Science, Sichuan University, Chengdu 610065, China
yzhang@scu.edu.cn
[2] College of Electrical Engineering, Sichuan University, Chengdu 610065, China
[3] Chengdu University of Information Technology, Chengdu 610225, China

Abstract. Magnetic resonance imaging (MRI) acquisition, reconstruction, and segmentation are usually processed independently in the conventional practice of MRI workflow. It is easy to notice that there are significant relevances among these tasks and this procedure artificially cuts off these potential connections, which may lead to losing clinically important information for the final diagnosis. To involve these potential relations for further performance improvement, a sequential multi-task joint learning network model is proposed to train a combined end-to-end pipeline in a differentiable way, aiming at exploring the mutual influence among those tasks simultaneously. Our design consists of three cascaded modules: 1) deep sampling pattern learning module optimizes the k-space sampling pattern with predetermined sampling rate; 2) deep reconstruction module is dedicated to reconstructing MR images from the undersampled data using the learned sampling pattern; 3) deep segmentation module encodes MR images reconstructed from the previous module to segment the interested tissues. The proposed model retrieves the latently interactive and cyclic relations among those tasks, from which each task will be mutually beneficial. The proposed framework is verified on MRB dataset, which achieves superior performance on other SOTA methods in terms of both reconstruction and segmentation. The code is available online: https://github.com/Deep-Imaging-Group/SemuNet.

Keywords: Fast MRI · Deep learning · Sampling learning · Image reconstruction · Segmentation

Electronic supplementary material The online version of this chapter (https://doi.org/10.1007/978-3-030-88552-6_8) contains supplementary material, which is available to authorized users.

N. Haq et al. (Eds.): MLMIR 2021, LNCS 12964, pp. 76–85, 2021.
https://doi.org/10.1007/978-3-030-88552-6_8

1   Introduction

Magnetic resonance imaging (MRI) is a non-invasive diagnostic imaging technique that enables studying low-contrast soft tissue structures without harmful radiation risk. However, its long acquisition time results in increasing costs, patient uncomfortableness, and motion artifacts. To conquer these obstacles, fast MRI acquisition is of great emergency. Nevertheless, simply reducing the sampling rate will degrade the imaging quality and jeopardize the sequential diagnosis. In the past decades, numerous efforts have made to recover high-quality MR images from undersampled k-space data, e.g., compressed sensing (CS) and later deep learning based methods. Inspite of fruitful results obtained, two defects can be sensed: 1) current undersampling patterns are empirically handtailored, e.g., radial, Cartesian, or Gaussian, which ignore the fact that different images may be suitable for different undersampling patterns; 2) suboptimal sampling pattern will lead to suboptimal reconstruction and finally impact the sequential analysis task. In summary, isolatedly handling the main steps in the whole imaging pipeline reveals the potential fact that both radiologists and computer aided intervention systems may be working with suboptimal reconstructed images.

Recently, in the field of signal processing, task driven methods, which directly train an end-to-end network and neglects the explicit intermediate result, have drawn increasingly attention. For examples, Bojarski et al. trained a self-driving network which learns commands directly from cameras without recogniting any landmarkers [1]. Liu et al. proposed to integrate the denoising network with a segmentation network to improve the denoising performance for segmentation [2]. Encouraged by these promising results, similar ideas were introduced into the field of medical imaging. Wu et al. and Lee et al., respectively proposed to detect the pulmonary nodules and intracranial hemorrhage diretly from the measured data without the step of image reconstruction [3,4]. In [5,6], the authors coupled MRI reconstruction with segmentation to improve the performance of both tasks. On the other hand, some recent studies attempted to optimize the k-space sampling patterns with a data-driven manner [7–9] and the optimized undersampling patterns show significant improvements, compared to empirical ones. Unfortunately, the scheme of these trajectories only learned from the reconstruction stage ignore the tissue of interest. Meanwhile, these methods mentioned above either combine the sampling and reconstruction, or joint the tasks of reconstruction and segmentation. None of the existing works consider the whole pipeline of medical image analysis, which means that useful information for final segmentation may be lost in each step.

To fully explore the mutual influence among sequential tasks and further improve the performance of each task simultaneously, in this study, we propose a sequential multi-task joint learning network framework (SemuNet), which jointly optimizes the sampling, reconstruction and segmentation in an end-to-end manner. The proposed framework can be divided into three modules: the sampling pattern learning network (SampNet), the reconstruction network (ReconNet), and the segmentation network (SegNet). Specifically, the well-known U-Net [10] is adopted as the backbone of our proposed ReconNet and SegNet for simplicity and, a probabilistic sampling network is proposed to learn the sampling pattern.

The remainder of this paper is organized as follows. The details of the proposed model, including each module, are elaborated in Sect. 2. The experimental results are presented and discussed in Sect. 3 and the final section concludes this paper.

2   Method

In this section, the main modules of the proposed framework SemuNet, including SampNet, ReconNet and SegNet, are first described sequentially in detail. Then other issues of the SemuNet, especially about the training strategy and loss function, are presented.

2.1   SampNet: The Sampling Pattern Learning Network

For the problem of CS-MR imaging, the task is to reconstruct an MR image from undersampled measurements in k-space, which approximates a fully-sampled MRI image $\mathbf{x} \in \mathbb{C}^{\sqrt{N} \times \sqrt{N}}$. Let $S_{\mathbf{T}_c}(\cdot)$ denotes the SampNet parameterized by $\mathbf{T}_c$, which outputs a $\sqrt{N} \times \sqrt{N}$ continuous value matrix (i.e., sampling pattern) as a partial observation in k-space. The undersampling process can be written as $S_{\mathbf{T}_c}(\mathbf{x}) \odot \mathbf{F}\mathbf{x}$, where $\odot$ is Hadamard product, $\mathbf{F}$ is the Fourier transform matrix. The goal of SampNet is to optimize the sampling pattern for specific datasets in the k-space. To learn a probabilistic observation matrix $\mathbf{T}_c$ in the k-space, we adopt the similar architecture to the [8,10,12] for our SampNet. The architecture of SampNet is shown in Fig. 1a. The details of SampNet is given in the supplementary material.

Since we do not have the labels for sampling pattern learning, we propose to merge the SampNet into the ReconNet and SegNet. When the cascaded network converges, the top-n largest values in $\mathbf{T}_c$ are replaced by Boolean values to produce the final sampling pattern $\mathbf{T}$, and n is chosen according to the predetermined sampling rate α , where $n = \alpha \cdot N$. Accordingly, the Booleanizing operation can be written defined as:

$$(\mathbf{T})_{ij} = \begin{cases} 1, & \text{if } (S_{\mathbf{T}_c}(\mathbf{x}))_{ij} \text{ is in top-}n, \\ 0, & \text{otherwise} \end{cases} \tag{1}$$

As a result, the pattern is optimized by the knowledge of both high-quality reconstructed images and accurate segmentation labels.

2.2   ReconNet: The Reconstruction Network

Recently, extensive network models were proposed for MRI reconstruction [13], and in this work, we simply utilize the spatial-domain based reconstruction network. Letting $R_\theta(\cdot)$ denote the ReconNet with parameter set θ, $\mathbf{F}^{-1}$ is the inverse Fourier transform matrix, the reconstructed image $\hat{\mathbf{x}}$ can be obtained as:

$$\tilde{\mathbf{x}} = R_\theta(\mathbf{F}^{-1}S_{\mathbf{T}_c}(\mathbf{x}) \odot \mathbf{Fx}) \qquad (2)$$

Then the training procedure can be formulated as the following optimization problem:

$$\{\theta^*, \mathbf{T}_c^*\} = \arg\min_{\theta, \mathbf{T}_c} \mathbb{E}_\mathbf{x}[g(R_\theta(\mathbf{F}^{-1}S_{\mathbf{T}_c}(\mathbf{x}) \odot \mathbf{Fx}), \mathbf{x})] \qquad (3)$$

where $g(\cdot)$ is a reconstruction metric function to measure the similarity between the reconstructed image and the label, and $\mathbb{E}_\mathbf{x}$ is the expectation over $\mathbf{x}$. The architecture of ReconNet adopts the well-known U-Net [10] as the backbone as shown in Fig. 1b, which has demonstrated competitive performance in artifact reduction for MRI [8,14].

2.3 SegNet: The Segmentation Network

Recently, lots of networks were proposed for automatic tissue segmentation [15]. Since U-Net like architecture has demonstrated excellent performance for medical image segmentation, in this part, we also choose the same network structure in Fig. 1b as our SegNet for simplicity. Then we can formulate the joint learning for simultaneously optimizing sampling, reconstruction and segmentation as follows

$$\{\epsilon^*, \theta^*, \mathbf{T}_c^*\} = \arg\min_{\epsilon, \theta, \mathbf{T}_c} \mathbb{E}_\mathbf{x}[g(R_\theta(\mathbf{F}^{-1}S_{\mathbf{T}_c}(\mathbf{x}) \odot \mathbf{Fx}), \mathbf{x})$$
$$+ h(H_\epsilon(R_\theta(\mathbf{F}^{-1}S_{\mathbf{T}_c}(\mathbf{x}) \odot \mathbf{Fx})), \mathbf{s})] \qquad (4)$$

where $h(\cdot)$ is the segmentation metric function to measure the segmentation accuracy of the result compared to the segmentation labels and $H_\epsilon(\cdot)$ is the segmentation network with parameter set ϵ.

The SegNet plays two roles. First, it is treated as a clinical analysis instructor to train ReconNet, such that the reconstruction network can better adapt to tissue segmentation work. Second, it serves as a radiologist, which can provide SampNet with sufficient clinical knowledge.

2.4 SemuNet: The Sequential Multi-task Joint Learning Network Framework

By cascading the previously mentioned SampNet, ReconNet and SegNet as the basic modules, we propose a deep joint learning framework for the whole MRI pipeline, which can: 1). learn an optimized sampling pattern simultaneously guided by both low- and high-level tasks, i.e. reconstruction and segmentation; 2). reconstruct high-quality MR images with the optimized sampling pattern for the downstream segmentation task; 3). and segment the target tissues more accurate based on the task-driven reconstruction.

Since these modules are cascaded and trained in an end-to-end manner, the features extracted from different tasks are mutually influenced in an interactive way and benefit from each other. The overview of the proposed joint learning network framework is illustrated in Fig. 1a and c. It can be seen that the networks in training and testing stages are different. During the training stage,

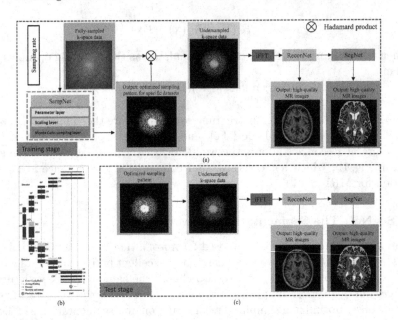

Fig. 1. Overview of the proposed joint learning network framework: SemuNet. (a) Training stage; (b) An encoder-decoder architecture; (c) Test stage.

since we need to learn the sampling pattern for the specific dataset with fully-sampled k-space data as labels, the whole framework has three parts. During the testing stage, since we can directly use the optimized sampling pattern to acquire the undersampled k-space data, SampNet is abandoned and the undersampled k-space data is fed into the ReconNet and SegNet in sequence. Finally, the estimated reconstruction and segmentation probability map are obtained.

Training Strategy. At the beginning of training stage, the whole network is initialized randomly. The cascaded modules are trained in an end-to-end manner, which updates the weights of three modules simultaneously using backpropagation. The reason to adopt such training strategy is to guarantee the learned sampling pattern can acquire the useful information as more as possible for the subsequent reconstruction and segmentation tasks. More specifically, the proposed SemuNet can be easily adapted to different clinical tasks and we can substitute the SegNet with any other task networks. Our approach not only facilitates the training effort while imposing ReconNet to fit clinical tasks and keeping SegNet performing accurately for undersampled MR images but also enables SampNet to learn more clinically useful features from the k-space data.

Loss Function. For MR images reconstruction, L_1 norm is adopted as the loss function:

$$\mathcal{L}^{Recon} = ||R_\theta(\mathbf{F}^{-1}S_{\mathbf{T}_c}(\mathbf{x}) \odot \mathbf{F}\mathbf{x}) - \mathbf{x}||_1 \qquad (5)$$

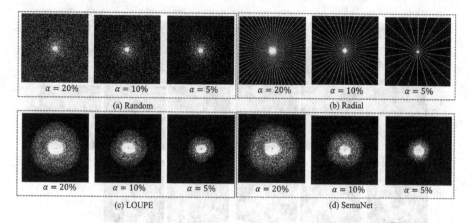

Fig. 2. Sampling patterns at different undersampling rates for MRB test dataset. (a) random and (b) radial patterns for Baseline, Liu et al. [2] and MD-Recon-Net [16]; (c) pattern learned by LOUPE [8]; (d) pattern learned by our SemuNet.

Cross-entropy loss is utilized for the SegNet:

$$\mathcal{L}^{Seg} = -\frac{1}{NC} \sum_{n=1}^{N} \sum_{c=1}^{C} t_{c,n}^{gt} \ln p_{c,n} \tag{6}$$

for C brain tissues class labels and N pixel number of an image, where $t_{c,n}^{gt}$ is the pixel-level target label and $p_{c,n}$ is the pixel-level Softmax segmentation probability for the cth class of the nth pixel. Then the hybrid loss function for the proposed joint learning network is formulated as:

$$\mathcal{L} = \mathcal{L}^{Recon} + \lambda \mathcal{L}^{Seg} \tag{7}$$

3 Experiments and Discussion

3.1 Experimental Details

Dataset and Baselines. The brain dataset from the Grand Challenge on MR Brain Image Segmentation workshop (MRB) [17] is used to evaluate the proposed method. The dataset is acquired using 3.0T MRI scan and consists of five patients. The dataset of each patient is provided with four MRI modalities: T1, T1-1mm, T1-IR and T2-FLAIR with size of $240 \times 240 \times 48$. The brain tissues of each patient are manually labeled with seven types of tissue (T1): cortical gray matter, basal ganglia, white matter, cerebrospinal fluid in the extracerebral space, ventricles, cerebellum, and brainstem. In our experiment, four T1 datasets are used for training and the remaining one for testing.

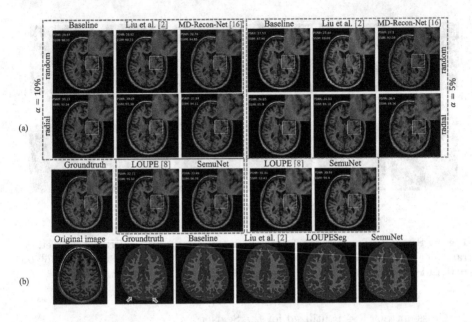

Fig. 3. (a) Reconstruction results of competing methods at different acceleration factors for MRB test dataset; (b) A brain tissue segmentation example from MRB test dataset (α = 5%) using different methods, the k-space data for Baseline and Liu et al. [2] are undersampled by random pattern.

Experiment Setup. All implementations are based on Pytorch. All models are trained using one Quadro RTX 8000 GPU and the batch size is set to 12. The hyperparameter configuration of both ReconNet and SegNet are given in Fig. 1b. Uniform random initialization is used for SampNet and Xavier initialization for ReconNet and SegNet. The whole SemuNet is trained for 600 epochs. After that, the ReconNet and SegNet are fine-tuned for additional 500 epochs. ADAM [18] optimizer is adopted with an initial learning rate of 10^{-4}. λ is empirically set to 10^{-1}.

Baseline. Two basic variants of our SemuNet framework are built: (1) Baseline = fixed pattern + ReconNet + SegNet; and (2) LOUPESeg = LOUPE + SegNet. LOUPE is a recently proposed sampling pattern learning model driven by reconstruction [8]. We first trained LOUPE with high quality MR images and then SegNet is trained with the data generated by LOUPE. PSNR and SSIM are adopted as quantitative metrics.

3.2   Experiments Results

To validate the performance of the proposed SemuNet, we separately evaluate the results of reconstruction and segmentation.

For reconstruction, we compare the proposed SemuNet with the following methods: (1) Baseline (only use its reconstruction result); (2) Liu et al. [2] with a fixed pattern (only use its reconstruction result); (3) LOUPE; (4) MD-Recon-Net [16] (a recently proposed dual-domain reconstruction network) with a fixed pattern. The learned trajectories for LOUPE and SemuNet, and the fixed patterns used in Baseline, Liu et al. [2] and MD-Recon-Net [16] are shown in Fig. 2a, respectively.

Table 1. MRI reconstruction results using PSNR (dB) and SSIM (%) of different methods on the MRB test dataset. The best result is shown in bold.

α	Metric	Baseline		Liu et al. [2]		MD-Recon-Net [16]		LOUPE [8]	SemuNet
		Radial	Random	Radial	Random	Radial	Random	Learned	Learned
20%	PSNR	36.30	32.69	36.17	32.81	**39.44**	39.34	38.82	39.24
	SSIM	96.67	94.01	96.24	93.76	98.09	97.80	98.09	**98.56**
10%	PSNR	31.30	30.26	31.14	30.31	32.62	33.95	33.63	**34.30**
	SSIM	90.27	90.69	90.93	90.73	93.59	94.47	95.19	**96.47**
5%	PSNR	27.45	28.95	27.26	28.87	26.83	30.12	30.96	**31.20**
	SSIM	85.00	88.46	84.45	88.54	85.13	92.00	91.31	**93.16**

Table 2. DSC (%) of different methods on the MRB test dataset The best result is shown in bold.

α	Baseline		Liu et al. [2]		LOUPE-Seg	SemuNet
	Random	Radial	Random	Radial		
20%	70.65	73.91	71.64	73.77	76.19	**76.79**
10%	68.3	70.48	67.73	70.92	72.91	**75.08**
5%	66.6	64.54	64.66	63.65	70.97	**72.45**

In Fig. 3a, one typical slice reconstructed using different methods is chosen for visual comparison. It can be observed that the proposed SemuNet achieves the minimal reconstruction error and preserves more details than other methods which can be confirmed in the magnified regions. The average values of the quantitative metrics on the 48 test data (from one patient) are listed in Table 1. It is noticed that our method achieves the highest scores in most situations, which can be seen as a powerful evidence of that integrating sampling learning and segmentation tasks can efficiently improve the reconstruction performance. In addition, we evaluate SemuNet on MRBrains18 [20] and fastMRI-Brain [21] (See supplementary material for more details).

As for segmentation, we compare our method with several methods: (1) Baseline; (2) LOUPESeg; and (3) Liu et al. [2]. The results of one representative slice are demonstrated in Fig. 3b. Each tissue is marked with a different color. It can be observed that the proposed SemuNet provides the most approximate visual result to the ground truth. Dice Similarity Coefficient (DSC) [19] is adopted as the quantitative metric and the results are list in Table 2. The quantitative results are consistent with the subjective evaluation, which confirm that introducing both sampling and reconstruction learning into segmentation network can further increase the accuracy. It is worth noting that the Baseline and Liu et al. [2] obtain much lower accuracy than other methods as shown in both Fig. 3b and Table 2, which shows the merit of undersampled MR image reconstruction with sampling learning as a preprocessing step for segmentation task. When we only apply sampling pattern learning without considering segmentation task, it also fails to achieve the highest accuracy since the reconstruction does not fully explore the latent features transferred from the segmentation task.

4   Limitation, Discussion and Conclusion

The proposed method has limitations in certain situation. First, the semantic information may not be fully mined in k-space when applying the model to other downstream because these tasks do not have as precise semantic information compared to segmentation tasks. Second, due to the expensive and private nature of medical labeling, it may be costly to produce downstream task labels for the dataset when applying the model to other body parts.

Sampling pattern learning is an important problem for MR imaging. With the recent developments of fast MRI in the industry, sampling pattern learning technique that takes both reconstruction and analysis tasks into account are of great significance. In this paper, a joint learning framework SemuNet, is proposed to integrate sampling pattern learning, reconstruction and segmentation into a unified network. The results demonstrate the joint learning strategy can benefit all the tasks from each other. In the future work, more datasets will used for evaluation and different analysis tasks will be considered.

References

1. Bojarski, M., et al.: End to end learning for self-driving cars. arXiv:1604.07316 [cs]. (2016)
2. Liu, D., Wen, B., Jiao, J., Liu, X., Wang, Z., Huang, T.S.: Connecting image denoising and high-level vision tasks via deep learning. IEEE Trans. Image Process. **29**, 3695–3706 (2020)
3. Wu, D., Kim, K., Dong, B., Fakhri, G.E., Li, Q.: End-to-end lung nodule detection in Computed tomography. In: Shi, Y., Suk, H.-I., Liu, M. (eds.) Mach. Learn. Med. Imaging, pp. 37–45. Springer International Publishing, Cham (2018)
4. Lee, H., Huang, C., Yune, S., Tajmir, S.H., Kim, M., Do, S.: Machine friendly machine learning: interpretation of computed tomography without image recon-struction. Sci. Rep. **9**, 15540 (2019)
5. Sun, L., Fan, Z., Ding, X., Huang, Y., Paisley, J.: Joint CS-MRI Reconstruction and Seg-mentation with a unified deep network. In: Chung, A.C.S., Gee, J.C., Yushkevich, P.A., Bao, S. (eds.) Inf. Process. Med. Imaging, pp. 492–504. Springer International Publishing, Cham (2019)

6. Fan, Z., Sun, L., Ding, X., Huang, Y., Cai, C., Paisley, J.: A segmentation-aware deep fusion network for compressed sensing MRI. In: Presented at the Proceedings of the European Conference on Computer Vision (ECCV) (2018)

7. Zijlstra, F., Viergever, M.A., Seevinck, P.R.: Evaluation of variable density and data-driven k-space undersampling for compressed sensing magnetic resonance imaging. Invest. Radiol. **51**, 410–419 (2016)

8. Bahadir, C.D., Dalca, A.V., Sabuncu, M.R.: Learning-based optimization of the under-sampling pattern in MRI. arXiv:1901.01960 [cs, eess, stat]. (2019)

9. Jin, K.H., Unser, M., Yi, K.M.: Self-supervised deep active accelerated MRI. arXiv:1901.04547 [cs]. (2019)

10. Ronneberger, O., Fischer, P., Brox, T.: U-Net: convolutional networks for biomedical image segmentation. In: Navab, N., Hornegger, J., Wells, W.M., Frangi, A.F. (eds.) MICCAI 2015. LNCS, vol. 9351, pp. 234–241. Springer, Cham (2015). https://doi.org/10.1007/978-3-319-24574-4_28

11. Jang, E., Gu, S., Poole, B.: Categorical reparameterization with Gumbel-Softmax. arXiv:1611.01144 [cs, stat]. (2017)

12. Maddison, C.J., Mnih, A., Teh, Y.W.: The concrete distribution: a continuous Relax-ation of discrete random variables. arXiv:1611.00712 [cs, stat]. (2017)

13. Wang, G., Ye, J.C., Mueller, K., Fessler, J.A.: Image reconstruction is a new frontier of machine learning. IEEE Trans. Med. Imaging. **37**, 1289–1296 (2018)

14. Yang, G., et al.: DAGAN: deep de-aliasing generative adversarial networks for fast compressed sensing MRI reconstruction. IEEE Trans. Med.l Imaging. **37**, 1310–1321 (2018)

15. Hesamian, M.H., Jia, W., He, X., Kennedy, P.: Deep learning techniques for medical image segmentation: achievements and challenges. J. Dig. Imaging **32**(4), 582–596 (2019). https://doi.org/10.1007/s10278-019-00227-x

16. Ran, M., et al.: MD-Recon-Net: a parallel dual-domain convolutional neural network for compressed sensing MRI. IEEE Trans. Radiat. Plasma Med. Sci. **5**, 120–135 (2021)

17. Mendrik, A.M., et al.: MRBrainS challenge: online evaluation framework for brain image segmentation in 3T MRI scans. Comput. Intell. Neurosci. **2015**, (2015)

18. Kingma, D.P., Ba, J.: Adam: a method for stochastic optimization. arXiv:1412.6980 [cs]. (2017)

19. Crum, W.R., Camara, O., Hill, D.L.G.: Generalized overlap measures for evaluation and validation in medical image analysis. IEEE Trans. Med. Imaging **25**, 1451–1461 (2006)

20. Kuijf, H.J., Bennink, E.: Grand challenge on MR brain segmentation at MICCAI (2018). http://mrbrains18.isi.uu.nl

21. Zbontar, J., et al.: fastMRI: an open dataset and benchmarks for accelerated MRI. arXiv:1811.08839 [physics, stat]. (2018)

Physics-Informed Self-supervised Deep Learning Reconstruction for Accelerated First-Pass Perfusion Cardiac MRI

Elena Martín-González[1]([✉])(ID), Ebraham Alskaf[2](ID), Amedeo Chiribiri[2](ID),
Pablo Casaseca-de-la-Higuera[1](ID), Carlos Alberola-López[1](ID), Rita G. Nunes[3](ID),
and Teresa Correia[2,4](ID)

[1] Laboratorio de Procesado de Imagen, ETSI Telecomunicación,
Universidad de Valladolid, Valladolid, Spain
`emargon@lpi.tel.uva.es`
[2] School of Biomedical Engineering and Imaging Sciences, King's College London,
London, UK
[3] Institute for Systems and Robotics, Department of Bioengineering,
Instituto Superior Técnico, Universidade de Lisboa, Lisbon, Portugal
[4] Centre for Marine Sciences - CCMAR, Faro, Portugal

Abstract. First-pass perfusion cardiac magnetic resonance (FPP-CMR) is becoming an essential non-invasive imaging method for detecting deficits of myocardial blood flow, allowing the assessment of coronary heart disease. Nevertheless, acquisitions suffer from relatively low spatial resolution and limited heart coverage. Compressed sensing (CS) methods have been proposed to accelerate FPP-CMR and achieve higher spatial resolution. However, the long reconstruction times have limited the widespread clinical use of CS in FPP-CMR. Deep learning techniques based on supervised learning have emerged as alternatives for speeding up reconstructions. However, these approaches require fully sampled data for training, which is not possible to obtain, particularly high-resolution FPP-CMR images. Here, we propose a physics-informed self-supervised deep learning FPP-CMR reconstruction approach for accelerating FPP-CMR scans and hence facilitate high spatial resolution imaging. The proposed method provides high-quality FPP-CMR images from 10x undersampled data without using fully sampled reference data.

Keywords: Deep learning reconstruction · Model-based reconstruction · Quantitative perfusion cardiac MRI

1 Introduction

Coronary artery disease (CAD) is the occlusion of the coronary arteries usually caused by atherosclerosis, which causes abnormalities in blood flow to the heart. Non-invasive imaging techniques that are used clinically for the evaluation of CAD are single photon emission computerized tomography (SPECT)

© Springer Nature Switzerland AG 2021
N. Haq et al. (Eds.): MLMIR 2021, LNCS 12964, pp. 86–95, 2021.
https://doi.org/10.1007/978-3-030-88552-6_9

and positron emission tomography (PET), but the reference for non-invasive myocardial perfusion quantification is PET [8]. However, the clinical value of first-pass perfusion cardiac magnetic resonance (FPP-CMR) has been shown in comparison to these techniques [6–8,20], having emerged as an alternative way of detecting blood flow anomalies without the use of potentially harmful ionising radiation. In addition, FPP-CMR has other advantages, such as higher spatial resolution, wider availability and lower scan cost compared to PET.

FPP-CMR time frames must be acquired in real-time to capture the rapid passage of a contrast agent bolus through the heart, and hence, the spatial resolution and coverage of the heart is compromised. Thus, undersampled reconstruction methods have been proposed to accelerate FPP-CMR acquisitions as a means to improve spatial resolution and heart coverage [14,16,21]. However, these methods can lead to long reconstruction times. In this work, we aim to speed up reconstructions and obtain the contrast-enhanced dynamic image series from undersampled FPP-CMR using deep learning (DL). Then, these images will be used to generate quantitative perfusion maps using a tracer kinetic model [4,9,11]. DL techniques have already been used in magnetic resonance image (MRI) reconstruction. Work has been reported on knee [2,13,22], brain [2,5,13,22] and cardiac [10,19] MRI, using both supervised [2,5,13] and self-supervised learning [15,22]. Occasionally, the network is unrolled to mimic a compressed sensing (CS) iterative reconstruction problem, giving rise to a cascade of convolutional neural networks (CNNs) [2,13,19]. The problem with supervised learning techniques is the need to have fully sampled reference images to train the network, which are not available in FPP-CMR, particularly at high spatial resolutions.

Even though the field of MRI reconstruction with DL is currently an active area, to our knowledge, self-supervised DL techniques have not been applied to FPP-CMR reconstruction. In this work, a SElf-supervised aCcelerated REconsTruction (SECRET) DL framework for FPP-CMR is proposed to directly reconstruct contrast-enhanced dynamic image series from undersampled (k, t)-space data.

2   Methods

For completeness, a conventional FPP-CMR CS reconstruction will be described. We will also describe our proposed method, SECRET, as well as the Model Based Deep Learning Architecture for Inverse Problems (MoDL) [2], which will be used for comparison.

2.1   Conventional FPP-CMR Reconstruction

CS methods can be used to reconstruct dynamic images from undersampled data. For example, FPP-CMR images **s** can be obtained from undersampled data $\mathbf{d}_u$ using CS by solving the following optimisation problem:

$$\hat{\mathbf{s}} = \arg\min_{\mathbf{s}}\{\|\mathbf{d}_u - \mathbf{E}\mathbf{s}\|_2^2 + \lambda_1\|\nabla_s\mathbf{s}\|_1 + \lambda_2\|\nabla_t\mathbf{s}\|_1\} \tag{1}$$

where $\mathbf{E} = \mathbf{A}\mathcal{F}$, $\mathbf{A}$ is the (k, t)-space sampling trajectory, $\mathcal{F}$ is the Fourier transform, λ_1 and λ_2 are regularization parameters and ∇_s and ∇_t are the finite differences operators along the spatial and temporal dimensions, respectively.

2.2   Supervised Learning Reconstruction: MoDL

MoDL combines the power of DL with model-based approaches [2]. It uses a CNN as a denoiser and applies it as a regulariser to solve the optimisation problem given by:

$$\mathbf{s}_{k+1} = \arg \min_{\mathbf{s}} \|\mathbf{d}_u - \mathbf{E}\mathbf{s}\|_2^2 + \lambda \|\mathbf{s} - \mathbf{z}_k\|_2^2 \tag{2}$$

$$\mathbf{s}_{k+1} = \left(\mathbf{E}^H \mathbf{E} + \lambda \mathcal{I}\right)^{-1} \left(\mathbf{E}^H \mathbf{d}_u + \lambda \mathbf{z}_k\right) \tag{3}$$

where k denotes the k-th iteration and $\mathbf{z}_k$ is the denoised version of $\mathbf{s}_k$, obtained through a CNN network. MoDL requires supervised learning to optimise the denoiser network. The data consistency layer is immediate by conjugate gradient blocks, but as the input is $\mathbf{z}_k$ and the output is $\mathbf{s}_{k+1}$, which, in turn, generates a $\mathbf{z}_{k+1}$, this requires iterating until convergence. The iterative algorithm is unrolled for a fixed number of iterations, K, in which the weights or parameters to be optimised are shared.

The MoDL method has the zero-filled reconstruction, the coil sensitivities and the subsampling mask as inputs, but it also needs the fully sampled images—which are hardly available for the case of FPP-CMR at high spatial resolution—for training. The loss is defined as the mean square error between s_K and the desired image t: $C = \sum_{i=1}^{N samples} \|\mathbf{s}_K(i) - \mathbf{t}(i)\|^2$, where $\mathbf{t}(i)$ is the i-th target image.

2.3   SECRET Reconstruction

The proposed SECRET method directly reconstructs contrast-enhanced dynamic images from the undersampled (k, t)-space data. Considering only the undersampled (k, t)-space data when enforcing data consistency, we can train networks without the need for fully sampled images, simply by making use of the physical models in the reconstruction [15]. This framework can be formulated as follows:

$$\hat{\theta} = \arg \min_{\theta} \|\mathbf{d}_u - \mathbf{A}\mathcal{F}C(\mathbf{s}_u|\theta)\|_2 \tag{4}$$

where $C(\mathbf{s}_u|\theta)$ is the output of a CNN, with θ the parameter vector to be optimised. Figure 1 shows the steps necessary for training our proposed SECRET method for FPP-CMR. First, undersampled (k, t)-space data $\mathbf{d}_u$ is transformed to the image domain, obtaining $\mathbf{s}_u$. Then, $\mathbf{s}_u$ enters the CNN to provide the reconstructed contrast-enhanced dynamic images $\hat{\mathbf{s}}$. These images are then transformed back to (k, t)-space $\hat{\mathbf{d}}$ and subsampling masks are applied, thus obtaining the undersampled version $\hat{\mathbf{d}}_u$. Finally, the loss is computed with $\hat{\mathbf{d}}_u$ and the input $\mathbf{d}_u$, to guide the training phase.

The CNN is based on the well-known U-Net [18], widely used in medical imaging. Skip connections are included to maintain information from previous layers, as well as to avoid the problem of vanishing gradients during backpropagation. At the end of the CNN, residual learning has been appended as in [15], adding the average image of the input $\mathbf{s}_u$.

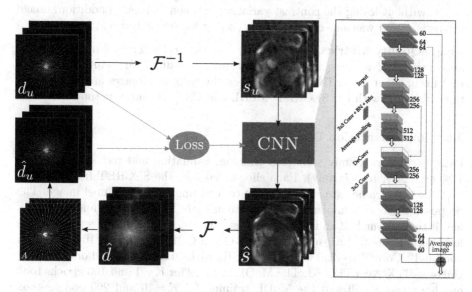

Fig. 1. Flow chart illustrating the proposed SECRET method for FPP-CMR. Blue lines represent steps that only take place during training. The inputs of the framework are the undersampled (k, t)-space data $\mathbf{d}_u$ and the (k, t)-sampling masks A, resulting in the reconstructed contrast-enhanced dynamic images $\hat{\mathbf{s}}$ as output, and $\hat{\mathbf{d}}_u$ if required. (Color figure online)

2.4 Dataset

Rest and stress FPP-CMR acquisitions were performed in 21 patients using a single-bolus injection of 0.05 mmol/kg Gadobutrol (Gadovist; Bayer, Germany) and a 1.5T CMR scanner (MAGNETOM Aera, Siemens Healthineers, Erlangen, Germany) with an 18-channel chest-coil and a 32-channel spine coil. A free-breathing FLASH perfusion dual-sequence [11] was used to acquire a low-resolution image with low T1-sensitivity for estimating the arterial input function and three short-axis slices (basal, mid and apical) for high resolution myocardial perfusion imaging using the following parameters: FOV $= 340 \times 308\,\mathrm{mm}^2$, in-plane resolution $= 2.2 \times 2.2\,\mathrm{mm}^2$, slice thickness $= 10\,\mathrm{mm}$, TR/TE $= 2.1/1\,\mathrm{ms}$, flip angle $= 8°$, parallel imaging acceleration factor 3, saturation recovery time $= 100\,\mathrm{ms}$, total scan duration $= 60\,\mathrm{s}$, contrast agent relaxivity $= 5.0\,\mathrm{L/mmol\ s}$. Undersampled datasets were generated for $3\times, 6\times$ and $10\times$ acceleration factors, following a radial (k, t)-sampling trajectory.

Preprocessing. A first step to ensure that all data had the same size, both spatially and temporally, prior to being fed to the CNN, consisted of resizing the DICOM images to obtain a spatial resolution of $2 \times 2\,mm^2$, padding the k-space to obtain an image size of 256×256 pixels, and interpolating each slice to a fixed number of frames (60 frames). A final step included intensity normalisation so that all contrast-enhanced dynamic image series present intensities between 0 and 1, without losing the contrast variation between frames. In addition, image pre-registration was also carried out to correct for respiratory motion.

Image Quality Metrics. Image quality was assessed in terms of peak signal-to-noise ratio (PSNR), structural similarity index measure (SSIM) and normalized root mean square error (NRMSE) between the reference images and reconstructions obtained with the SECRET, MoDL and CS (10× only) methods.

2.5   Implementation Details

Patients were randomly split into training, validation and test subsets (60%, 16% and 24%, respectively). Each slice is fed into the SECRET framework so that the time frames are stacked in depth, creating a multi-channel image. The proposed method is implemented in Python with Tensorflow [1] and Keras [3], and it took about half an hour of training using the Adam optimizer [12] with a learning rate of 10^{-4} consuming about 3 GB of GPU memory for 100 epochs on one Intel® Core™ i7-4790 CPU @ 3.60 GHz with 16 GB RAM and one NVIDIA GeForce RTX 2080 Ti GPU. The MoDL training for $K = 1$ and 100 epochs took one hour and a half and the MoDL training for $K = 10$ and 200 epochs took forty-five hours using the same hardware. Note that after training the SECRET method, it provides a reconstruction of a complete contrast-enhanced dynamic image series in less than a second.

3   Results and Discussion

Figure 2 shows the SECRET reconstructions obtained for two representative patients from 6× and 10× undersampled (k, t)-space data together with the reference and MoDL ($K = 1$) reconstructions. CS reconstruction is also shown for 10×. Three different time frames are shown, corresponding to right ventricle (RV), left ventricle (LV) and myocardial enhancement. Although the SECRET reconstructions are slightly blurred, due to residual learning from the average image of the CNN input (which is blurred due to residual motion), it can be seen that they have better quality than the images obtained with MoDL trained in the same amount of time. Moreover, SECRET images maintain the variability of contrast that exists between frames in addition to not losing the structure of the heart.

Figure 3 shows results of the FPP-CMR reconstructions in terms of PSNR, SSIM and NRMSE. While the performance of MoDL becomes noticeably worse as the acceleration rate increases, SECRET maintains good image quality even at high acceleration rates. For the 10× accelerated reconstructions, the **median**

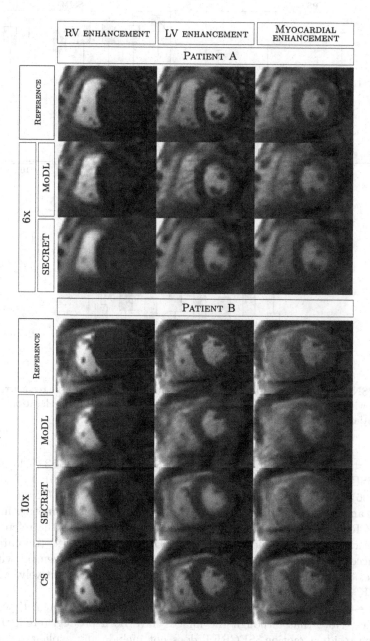

Fig. 2. SECRET and MoDL ($K = 1$) reconstructions obtained from $6\times$ and $10\times$ undersampled FPP-CMR data for two representative subjects. The reference images are displayed for comparison, in addition to CS reconstruction for $10\times$. The right ventricle (RV), left ventricle (LV) and myocardial enhancement time frames are shown for one short axis slice.

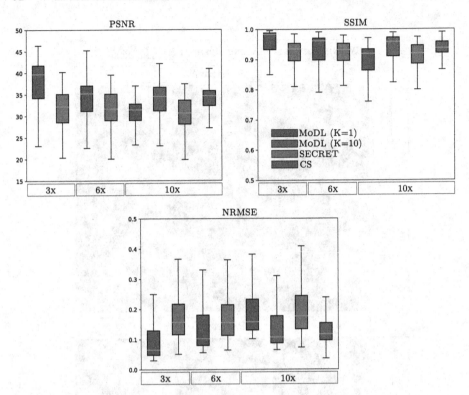

Fig. 3. PSNR, SSIM and NRMSE between the reference images and the reconstructions obtained with SECRET and MoDL methods, for 3×, 6× and 10× acceleration factors, for all patients in the test dataset.

(interquartile range): PSNR was **34.66** (3.47), **31.46** (3.81), **34.52** (5.43), **30.67** (5.52); SSIM was **0.94** (0.04), **0.92** (0.07), **0.96** (0.06), **0.92** (0.06); NRMSE was **0.12** (0.06), **0.16** (0.10), **0.11** (0.09), **0.17** (0.11) for CS, MoDL (K = 1), MoDL (K = 10) and SECRET methods, respectively. The image quality metrics indicate that SECRET images maintain a more stable agreement with the reference as the acceleration factor is increased than MoDL images, which deteriorate with higher acceleration. CS and MoDL (K = 10) show the best agreement with the reference, but reconstructions take ∼87.08 s and ∼1.99 s, respectively, whereas MoDL (K = 1) takes ∼0.21 s and SECRET only 0.15 s.

Figure 4 shows a 1D projection of the dynamic images through time, for a given slice. Note that although the images have been pre-registered, there is still some residual motion. SECRET does not include any explicit regularisation term, however, due to the residual learning performed by the network all reconstructions provided by the framework are inherently corrected. Such good PSNR, SSIM and NRMSE values obtained when the reference images are affected by little respiratory motion, would certainly improve if some regularisation were added. This would enable even higher acceleration rates. Regularisation schemes will thus be investigated in a future study.

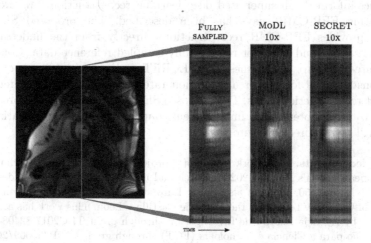

Fig. 4. Representative image profile across the heart demonstrating that the SECRET framework improves consistency across time frames.

Quantitative parameter maps were estimated from the FPP-CMR reconstructions, showing the potential of the technique for an objective and operator-independent analysis of myocardial perfusion. Figure 5 displays the contrast transfer coefficient (K^{Trans}) map estimated from fully sampled, 6× and 10× undersampled patient data using the MoDL and SECRET methods, through the Patlak model [17]. The image quality of the quantitative maps obtained from the SECRET reconstruction at accelerations 6× and 10× is comparable to the reference images, showing less blurring than MoDL maps.

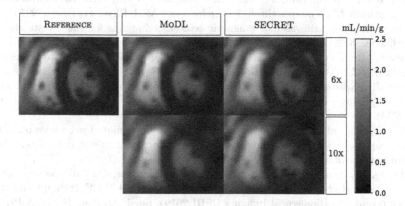

Fig. 5. Quantitative maps (K^{Trans}) obtained from 6× and 10× undersampled data using MoDL and the SECRET methods. The reference image is displayed for comparison.

4 Conclusion

A physics-informed self-supervised deep learning reconstruction framework for accelerating FPP-CMR scans has been described. The proposed SECRET method provides FPP-CMR reconstructions directly from the undersampled (k, t)-space data and does not require fully sampled reference data. Compared with state-of-the-art approaches, the SECRET method maintains good quality reconstructions for higher acceleration rates, with low training times and very fast reconstruction times. The proposed SECRET method shows promising results, with the potential for improvement coupled with explicit regularization, which will be explored in future work.

Acknowledgements. This work is part of a project that has received funding from the European Union's Horizon 2020 research and innovation programme under grant agreement No 867450. Authors also thank European Social Fund, Operational Programme of Castilla y León, and the Junta de Castilla y León. This work has also been supported by Agencia Estatal de Investigación through grant TEC2017-82408-R and by Fundação para a Ciência e Tecnologia (FCT) through grant UIDP/50009/2020.

References

1. Abadi, M., et al.: TensorFlow: large-scale machine learning on heterogeneous systems (2015). https://www.tensorflow.org/. Software available from tensorflow.org
2. Aggarwal, H.K., Mani, M.P., Jacob, M.: MoDL: model-based deep learning architecture for inverse problems. IEEE Trans. Med. Imaging **38**(2), 394–405 (2018)
3. Chollet, F., et al.: Keras (2015). https://keras.io
4. Correia, T., Schneider, T., Chiribiri, A.: Model-based reconstruction for highly accelerated first-pass perfusion cardiac MRI. In: Shen, D., et al. (eds.) MICCAI 2019. LNCS, vol. 11765, pp. 514–522. Springer, Cham (2019). https://doi.org/10.1007/978-3-030-32245-8_57
5. Do, W.J., Seo, S., Han, Y., Ye, J.C., Choi, S.H., Park, S.H.: Reconstruction of multicontrast MR images through deep learning. Med. Phys. **47**(3), 983–997 (2020)
6. Foley, J.R.J.: Cardiovascular magnetic resonance imaging for the investigation of ischaemic heart disease. Ph.D. thesis, University of Leeds (2018)
7. Hendel, R.C., et al.: CMR first-pass perfusion for suspected inducible myocardial ischemia. JACC Cardiovasc. Imaging **9**(11), 1338–1348 (2016)
8. Heo, R., Nakazato, R., Kalra, D., Min, J.K.: Noninvasive imaging in coronary artery disease. In: Seminars in Nuclear Medicine, vol. 44, pp. 398–409. Elsevier (2014)
9. Hsu, L.Y., et al.: Diagnostic performance of fully automated pixel-wise quantitative myocardial perfusion imaging by cardiovascular magnetic resonance. JACC Cardiovasc. Imag. **11**(5), 697–707 (2018)
10. Huang, Q., Yang, D., Wu, P., Qu, H., Yi, J., Metaxas, D.: MRI reconstruction via cascaded channel-wise attention network. In: 2019 IEEE 16th International Symposium on Biomedical Imaging (ISBI 2019), pp. 1622–1626. IEEE (2019)
11. Kellman, P., et al.: Myocardial perfusion cardiovascular magnetic resonance: optimized dual sequence and reconstruction for quantification. J. Cardiovasc. Magn. Reson. **19**(1), 1–14 (2017)

12. Kingma, D.P., Ba, J.: Adam: a method for stochastic optimization. arXiv preprint arXiv:1412.6980 (2014)
13. Kocanaogullari, D., Eksioglu, E.M.: Deep learning for MRI reconstruction using a novel projection based cascaded network. In: 2019 IEEE 29th International Workshop on Machine Learning for Signal Processing (MLSP), pp. 1–6. IEEE (2019)
14. Lingala, S.G., Hu, Y., DiBella, E., Jacob, M.: Accelerated dynamic MRI exploiting sparsity and low-rank structure: KT SLR. IEEE Trans. Med. Imaging **30**(5), 1042–1054 (2011)
15. Liu, F., Kijowski, R., El Fakhri, G., Feng, L.: Magnetic resonance parameter mapping using model-guided self-supervised deep learning. Magn. Reson. Med. **85**, 3211–3226 (2021)
16. Otazo, R., Kim, D., Axel, L., Sodickson, D.K.: Combination of compressed sensing and parallel imaging for highly accelerated first-pass cardiac perfusion MRI. Magn. Reson. Med. **64**(3), 767–776 (2010)
17. Patlak, C.S., Blasberg, R.G., Fenstermacher, J.D.: Graphical evaluation of blood-to-brain transfer constants from multiple-time uptake data. J. Cereb. Blood Flow Metab. **3**(1), 1–7 (1983)
18. Ronneberger, O., Fischer, P., Brox, T.: U-Net: convolutional networks for biomedical image segmentation. In: Navab, N., Hornegger, J., Wells, W.M., Frangi, A.F. (eds.) MICCAI 2015. LNCS, vol. 9351, pp. 234–241. Springer, Cham (2015). https://doi.org/10.1007/978-3-319-24574-4_28
19. Schlemper, J., Caballero, J., Hajnal, J.V., Price, A.N., Rueckert, D.: A deep cascade of convolutional neural networks for dynamic MR image reconstruction. IEEE Trans. Med. Imaging **37**(2), 491–503 (2017)
20. Schwitter, J., et al.: MR-IMPACT II: magnetic resonance imaging for myocardial perfusion assessment in coronary artery disease trial: perfusion-cardiac magnetic resonance vs. single-photon emission computed tomography for the detection of coronary artery disease: a comparative multicentre, multivendor trial. Eur. Heart J. **34**(10), 775–781 (2013)
21. Vitanis, V., et al.: High resolution three-dimensional cardiac perfusion imaging using compartment-based K-T principal component analysis. Magn. Reson. Med. **65**(2), 575–587 (2011)
22. Yaman, B., et al.: Self-supervised learning of physics-guided reconstruction neural networks without fully sampled reference data. Magn. Reson. Med. **84**(6), 3172–3191 (2020)

Deep Learning for General Image Reconstruction

Noise2Stack: Improving Image Restoration by Learning from Volumetric Data

Mikhail Papkov[1]([✉]), Kenny Roberts[2], Lee Ann Madissoon[2], Jarrod Shilts[2], Omer Bayraktar[2], Dmytro Fishman[1], Kaupo Palo[3], and Leopold Parts[1,2]

[1] Institute of Computer Science, University of Tartu, Tartu, Estonia
mikhail.papkov@ut.ee
[2] Wellcome Sanger Institute, Hinxton, UK
[3] PerkinElmer Inc., Tallinn, Estonia

Abstract. Biomedical images are noisy. The imaging equipment itself has physical limitations, and the consequent experimental trade-offs between signal-to-noise ratio, acquisition speed, and imaging depth exacerbate the problem. Denoising is, therefore, an essential part of any image processing pipeline, and convolutional neural networks are currently the method of choice for this task. One popular approach, Noise2Noise, does not require clean ground truth, and instead, uses a second noisy copy as a training target. Self-supervised methods, like Noise2Self and Noise2Void, learn the signal without an explicit target, but are limited by the lack of information in a single image. Here, we introduce Noise2Stack, an extension of the Noise2Noise method to image stacks that takes advantage of a shared signal between spatially neighboring planes. Our experiments on magnetic resonance brain scans and multiplane microscopy data show that learning only from image neighbors in a stack is sufficient to outperform Noise2Noise and Noise2Void and close the gap to supervised denoising methods. Our findings point to a low-cost, high-reward improvement in denoising pipelines of multiplane biomedical images.

Keywords: Denoising · Microscopy · Magnetic resonance imaging

1 Introduction and Related Work

Noise is inevitable in biological and medical imaging. Equipment imperfection in microscopy leads to image artifacts, some signal frequencies are undersampled in magnetic resonance scans, exposure time is restricted to capture dynamic information, or to avoid sample bleaching and phototoxicity. Therefore, image analysis in medicine and biology often relies on reconstruction. Its primary objective

Electronic supplementary material The online version of this chapter (https://doi.org/10.1007/978-3-030-88552-6_10) contains supplementary material, which is available to authorized users.

N. Haq et al. (Eds.): MLMIR 2021, LNCS 12964, pp. 99–108, 2021.
https://doi.org/10.1007/978-3-030-88552-6_10

is to approximate clean image signal $s = s' + x$ by recovering absent information s' from the acquired image x, or decomposing the acquisition $x = s + n$ into signal s and degrading noise n.

Deep learning advances have improved image restoration [1,4,9,10,12,21]. Convolutional neural networks are currently outperforming traditional (non-trainable) methods such as non-local means [3] or BM3D [5] in open benchmarks [13], e.g. in fluorescence microscopy denoising [23]. From deep learning point of view, the most intuitive way to approach the task is to train a neural network to reconstruct the clean target from the noisy image. This approach is often referred to as Noise2Clean. During the training, network parameters are optimized to minimize the error between predicted signal $\hat{s}$ and true signal s. However, acquiring clean ground truth is challenging, often requiring multiple measurements and their subsequent registration [21,23].

It is possible to train a denoising network without clean ground truth by providing two independently corrupted versions (i.e. multiple acquisitions) of the same image, as was proposed by Lehtinen et al. [12]. Noise2Noise uses these corrupted versions both as input and target to reconstruct the signal across various noise types and image domains including magnetic resonance imaging (MRI) scans [12]. This approach is justified by an assumption that the network learns the expected value of target pixels. One of its main limitations is the requirement to have two independently corrupted copies of the data. While it is straightforward to synthetically corrupt ground truth images twice, acquiring two independent measurements is usually not done.

To mitigate this requirement, multiple methods were developed to train a denoising network from a single measurement. Noise2Void [9] and Noise2Self [1] exploited the idea that the signal is not pixel-wise independent, but the noise is conditionally pixel-wise independent given the signal. Both methods approximate a blind-spot architecture by masking procedure which reduces training efficiency [11] and makes the system susceptible to structured noise. Further work has improved on this result by estimating the parameters of the noise distribution [10], using predefined noise model [17], extending the blind mask according to noise autocorrelation [2], and introducing a masking-free approach [11].

While extended approaches dominated traditional training-free denoising algorithms, they could not outperform supervised methods. This motivates using more data during training instead. In medical imaging, it is common to have a stack of 2D planes that could be combined in a single volumetric image. For MRI, these planes are resonance signals from a certain sample depth [15], for cell microscopy, acquisitions from consecutive focal planes [6]. It may be possible to take advantage of similarity between neighboring planes and denoise an image stack from self. One can split a stack of planes in half, and train a network to predict even planes using odd and vice versa [4,22]. Although it is beneficial when only one data copy is available, the number of training examples in this case decreases to the number of available image stacks, which often is a strict limiting factor in neural network training. The same issue arises when using 3D networks additionally to the increased computational costs.

In this work, we present Noise2Stack, an extension of the Noise2Noise model that makes use of information from the neighbouring planes to improve the quality of the image denoising (Figs. 2 and 4). Our experiments demonstrate that Noise2Stack trained on neighbouring planes in addition to the copy of the target image, consistently outperforms the original Noise2Noise method. Moreover, we show that even without noisy copy of the target image, its performance matches or even exceeds the one of Noise2Noise method. Such training scheme allows learning from a single stack of 2D images without requiring the second independently corrupted copy, which is often hard or impossible to acquire.

2   Methods

Noise2Stack (Fig. 1) is a sampling algorithm for training denoising neural networks which selects a set of planes from a provided stack on each step. It can operate in two modes. In the *copy-supervised mode*, a copy of the reconstructed plane is passed as an input along with its neighbors. Without adding neighbouring planes, this is equivalent to the original Noise2Noise strategy. In the second, *self-supervised mode*, the reconstructed plane is held out as a training target and not used as input. For an even number of input planes, the self-supervised mode was used. *E.g.* with two-plane training, to denoise the i-th plane, only its neighbors $i + 1$ and $i - 1$ were used. For odd numbers of planes, the copy-supervised mode was used: the i-th plane was also a part of the input.

In both modes, we train a single denoising neural network for all the planes, ignoring their absolute spatial location in a stack. Note that for the self-supervised mode, we do not require two independently corrupted copies of a stack. Instead, we use just a single noisy stack, predicting each image plane using its neighbors. For the marginal planes, we replace their absent neighbors with copies of their nearest neighbor plane.

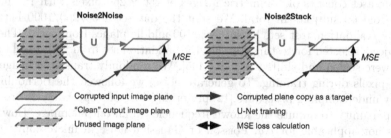

Fig. 1. Noise2Noise and Noise2Stack training strategies. Noise2Noise uses two independently corrupted copies of each image plane (blue copy as an input, red copy as a target). For Noise2Stack we can choose whether to show reconstructed plane to the network as an input along with its neighbors (two neighbors training illustrated). (Color figure online)

Neural Network Architecture. Most of the previously proposed deep learning denoising methods [9, 12] are training strategies which can be used with any suitable backbone. Noise2Stack is no exception; the only architectural aspect to modify when adopting a new backbone is the number of input planes. We used previously published variations of a U-Net [20] that were applied to similar tasks. For MRI denoising, we used a Noise2Noise architecture [12], and for microscopy denoising, we adopted a network from CSBDeep framework [21]. Both of them were implemented using PyTorch [18].

Training. In all experiments, the neural network was trained for 100 epochs with batch size 16 on a single NVIDIA V100 GPU. The network was optimized using Adam [8] algorithm with initial learning rate 10^{-3} and default parameters $\beta_1 = 0.9$, $\beta_2 = 0.999$, $\epsilon = 10^{-8}$ without weight decay. The learning rate was decreasing every epoch according to the cosine schedule [14]. We used mean squared error (MSE) loss function which was computed directly on the network output without additional post-processing steps.

3   Experiments

We evaluated our Noise2Stack method against several baselines on two multiplane datasets from different domains: IXI brain scan MRI T1 dataset[1] and microscopy dataset in brightfield and fluorescence modalities [19].

We used peak signal-to-noise ratio (PSNR) as a primary metric to compare our results with previous reports [12]. In addition, we measured structural similarity index (SSIM) and normalized root mean squared error (NRMSE). For fluorescence microscopy images, before measuring metrics we applied percentile normalization between 0.1 and 99.9 and an affine transformation to minimize MSE between predictions and ground truth [21]. Results are summarized in Table 1.

3.1   MRI

MRI dataset consists of volumetric images of 256×256 pixels with 150 planes each, from 60 subjects in total. We split the dataset 4800/200/1000 between training/validation/test sets by subject (100 middle planes from each). The list of subjects selected for testing matches the validation set from [12]. Pixel intensities were scaled and shifted to $[-0.5, 0.5]$. We randomly translated images by $[0, 64]$ pixels during training. To generate noise, we followed the Bernoulli frequency undersampling procedure [12] preserving 10% of a spectrum. It provides an opportunity to impute the known frequencies in an output image. However, this is not applicable for *e.g.* Poisson or Gaussian noise in microscopy, so we treat it as a post-processing step rather than a part of end-to-end training. We report the performance both before and after post-processing for MRI.

We measured the baseline performance on the whole test set for direct inverse fast Fourier transform reconstruction of undersampled spectra [12]. Our test set had an average PSNR of 20.7 dB for directly reconstructed images. When two input images spectra are combined, mean PSNR rises to 22.4 dB.

First, we replicated the previous results [12]. A single plane Noise2Noise model increases PSNR to 29.1 (30.9 with post-processing). Our *test* set results

---

[1] http://biomedic.doc.ic.ac.uk/brain-development/downloads/IXI/IXI-T1.tar.

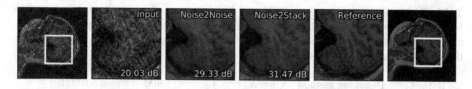

Fig. 2. Example result of Noise2Stack MRI denoising compared to Noise2Noise, input image and reference.

for the original Noise2Noise strategy are slightly (0.8 dB) worse than previously reported on the *validation* set, which is consistent with expectation.

Adding four neighbors to the Noise2Noise input in copy-supervised mode increased PSNR by 1.8 dB both before and after post-processing (Fig. 2). Limiting the number of neighbouring planes to four (two from each side) proved optimal, resulting in the greatest performance benefits in both modes. Using a single image stack for training in a self-supervised mode with four neighbours in the input, we outperform the original Noise2Noise model by 0.8 dB.

Next, we investigated whether position in the stack affected denoising performance. We evaluated the best trained model across different plane locations and found that the marginal planes have higher PSNR after the reconstruction as well as for the baseline (Fig. 3A).

3.2 Microscopy

Microscopy dataset [19] consists of 270 pairs of low-exposure (20 ms, noisy) and high-exposure (100 ms, clean) fluorescence modality images and 270 respective brightfield images of size 2160×2160 pixels. Each image contains ten focal planes separated by 2 μm in z-stack. We split them 180/30/60 between training/validation/test sets by well and cell line. Before training, the global background pattern (pixel-wise median across all images in modality) was subtracted from each image before normalization between 3 and 99.8 percentiles [21]. During training, images were randomly rotated by $90 \times N$ degrees, flipped both horizontally and vertically, and cropped to 256×256 pixels.

We compared Noise2Stack with a supervised denoising method, which used low-exposure images as inputs and high-exposure images as training targets. The second stack of low-exposure images was not available, therefore, training Noise2Noise network was not possible. In addition, we evaluated our strategy against another self-supervised method, Noise2Void [9], which does not require a noise model, does not put any restrictions on volumetric data properties, and treats all the planes independently of their position in the stack. For the training, we used the default Noise2Void configuration recommended by the authors, since autocorrelation map did not reveal the noise structure [2]. As a baseline, we used the unsupervised BM3D denoising algorithm [5, 16]. To maximize its performance, we supplied it with the true noise standard deviation of 0.008 measured against high-exposure images scaled to [0, 1].

Table 1. Model performance on MRI and fluorescence cell microscopy datasets. For MRI, metrics were measured against clean image copy without synthetic noise. For microscopy, metrics were measured against a ground truth sample. Average results before and after post-processing are shown alongside.

Dataset	Denoising method	N input	PSNR ↑		SSIM ↑		NRMSE ↓	
		Planes	Before	After	Before	After	Before	After
MRI	–	–	20.7	22.4	0.38	0.43	0.244	0.201
	Noise2Noise	1	29.1	30.9	0.85	0.87	0.092	0.075
	Noise2Stack	1+2	30.3	32.2	0.88	0.90	0.080	0.064
	(copy-supervised)	1+4	30.9	32.7	0.89	0.91	0.075	0.061
		1+6	30.8	32.6	0.89	0.91	0.075	0.061
	Noise2Stack	2	28.6	31.3	0.84	0.87	0.097	0.072
	(self-supervised)	4	29.2	31.7	0.85	0.88	0.091	0.069
		6	29.0	31.5	0.85	0.87	0.093	0.070
Microscopy	–	–	25.8		0.40		0.388	
	BM3D	1	31.0'		0.68		0.222	
	Noise2Clean	1	32.8		0.77		0.174	
	Noise2Void	1	26.8		0.44		0.357	
	Noise2Stack	2	31.6		0.73		0.195	
	(self-supervised)	4	31.6		0.73		0.197	

High-exposure fluorescence images were used as a ground truth when denoising low-exposure images in supervised way and calculating metrics. We only evaluated the results visually for the brightfield images, since they are available in a single exposure. Figure 3B illustrates PSNR for different models as well as for raw images with respect to the plane position in a stack. In both Figs. 3 and 4 we showed denoising results obtained using two neighbouring planes as input. Figure 4 shows visual comparison of the denoising results with noisy and clean microscopy images. Noise2Stack was able to capture the signal in a self-supervised way, achieving PSNR 31.6 dB and producing visually almost as good results as supervised Noise2Clean, although 1.2 dB less by PSNR. Both Noise2Stack and Noise2Clean outperformed the BM3D and Noise2Void baselines in our experiments.

To demonstrate the applicability of Noise2Stack as a general first step in the image analysis pipeline, we segmented fluorescence microscopy images with a pre-trained neural network [7]. Images were segmented independently of their position in the stack one by one without any aggregation, because small nuclei could appear in lower planes and vanish in upper ones or vice versa. Ground truth segmentation is not available for this dataset, so we visually evaluated the consistency of predictions and the amount of artifacts introduced by noise. Large-scale manual expert curation and subsequent numerical evaluation are beyond the scope of this work. In Fig. 4 we show semantic segmentation probability maps for low-exposure, denoised, and high-exposure images. We observed the biggest

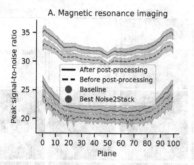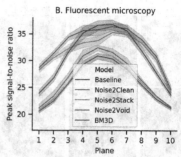

Fig. 3. The impact of plane location on model performance. **A:** average peak signal-to-noise ratio on the test set of MRI dataset (y-axis), ranging the target plane location across the 100 available ones (x-axis). Red: baseline (direct inverse Fourier transform); blue: copy-supervised Noise2Stack with five input planes (two neighbors from each side); error band: 95% confidence interval for 10 subjects. **B:** average peak signal-to-noise ratio on the test set of fluorescent microscopy dataset (y-axis), ranging the target plane location across the 10 available ones (x-axis). Red: baseline (low-exposure image); other colors: models in comparison; error band: 95% confidence interval for 6 stacks. (Color figure online)

impact of denoising algorithms in marginal planes, where signal-to-noise ratio was the lowest.

4 Discussion

Noise2Stack was motivated by the observation of neighboring plane similarity in volumetric biomedical datasets. *E.g.* for MRI brain scan dataset, the average SSIM between neighboring planes is 0.86. We showed that U-Net is able to capture this similarity and use it for denoising. In both copy-supervised (where the original Noise2Noise belongs) and self-supervised modes, four neighbors were optimal for denoising of MRI, and two were best for microscopy. We hypothesize that the number of planes depends on the physical distance between imaged planes, and that the optimum differs between datasets. However, it is clear that further planes provide less useful information for the restoration and could lead to network overfitting.

The marginal planes in MRI data have higher PSNR for both baseline and denoised images. Conversely, middle planes have the highest quality in microscopy (Fig. 3). Despite this difference, Noise2Stack demonstrated stable performance improvement over methods that do not use information from the neighbouring planes. Unsupervised BM3D algorithm showed good results for the middle microscopy planes, however failed in the marginal ones with lower signal-to-noise ratio (Fig. 3B). In complex conditions, it produced a number of artifacts that corrupted the downstream segmentation results (Figs. 4, S1 in supplementary material). In our experiments, it was also 700 times slower than all of the considered deep learning methods which have comparable throughput.

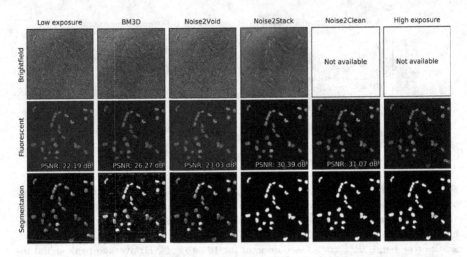

Fig. 4. Microscopy denoising results compared to low-exposure and high-exposure images in fluorescence and brightfield modalities (the second plane from the fourth test stack was taken as an illustrative example). Segmentation of fluorescence images with a pre-trained neural network illustrates denoising effects on downstream analysis; red: probability map thresholded by 0.5 and cleaned. (Color figure online)

The level of detail in MRI denoised with Noise2Stack in copy-supervised mode was noticeably increased compared to Noise2Noise (Figs. 2, S2 in supplementary material). Self-supervised mode expectedly produced less detailed output. However, this mode demands only half the data compared to Noise2Noise without any performance loss. For fluorescence microscopy, self-supervised Noise2Stack had similar performance to Noise2Clean.

5   Conclusion

We introduced Noise2Stack, a simple approach to improve denoising results for volumetric data by using neighboring planes as an additional source of information. Further, we exapted the blind-spot idea [1, 9] to the multiplane case without the masking approximation. This practical extension achieved supervised level of performance with a single image stack, reducing imaging times, or avoiding additional assumptions about the noise characteristics.

Noise2Stack can be applied in domains where measurements are made in a spatially structured manner. The limitations of sampling to secure the required amount of shared signal between acquisitions is a subject of further studies.

Acknowledgments. This work was funded by PerkinElmer Inc. (VLTAT19682) and Wellcome Trust (206194). We thank High Performance Computing Center of the Institute of Computer Science at the University of Tartu for the provided computing power.

References

1. Batson, J., Royer, L.: Noise2Self: blind denoising by self-supervision. In: International Conference on Machine Learning, pp. 524–533. PMLR (2019)
2. Broaddus, C., Krull, A., Weigert, M., Schmidt, U., Myers, G.: Removing structured noise with self-supervised blind-spot networks. In: 2020 IEEE 17th International Symposium on Biomedical Imaging (ISBI), pp. 159–163. IEEE (2020)
3. Buades, A., Coll, B., Morel, J.M.: Non-local means denoising. Image Process. On Line **1**, 208–212 (2011)
4. Buchholz, T.O., Jordan, M., Pigino, G., Jug, F.: Cryo-care: content-aware image restoration for cryo-transmission electron microscopy data. In: 2019 IEEE 16th International Symposium on Biomedical Imaging (ISBI 2019), pp. 502–506. IEEE (2019)
5. Dabov, K., Foi, A., Katkovnik, V., Egiazarian, K.: Image denoising by sparse 3-d transform-domain collaborative filtering. IEEE Trans. Image Process. **16**(8), 2080–2095 (2007)
6. Dalgarno, P.A., et al.: Multiplane imaging and three dimensional nanoscale particle tracking in biological microscopy. Opt. Express **18**(2), 877–884 (2010)
7. Fishman, D., et al.: Segmenting nuclei in brightfield images with neural networks. bioRxiv p. 764894 (2019)
8. Kingma, D.P., Ba, J.: Adam: a method for stochastic optimization (2017)
9. Krull, A., Buchholz, T.O., Jug, F.: Noise2Void-learning denoising from single noisy images. In: Proceedings of the IEEE Conference on Computer Vision and Pattern Recognition, pp. 2129–2137 (2019)
10. Krull, A., Vičar, T., Prakash, M., Lalit, M., Jug, F.: Probabilistic Noise2Void: unsupervised content-aware denoising. Front. Comput. Sci. **2**, 5 (2020)
11. Laine, S., Karras, T., Lehtinen, J., Aila, T.: High-quality self-supervised deep image denoising. arXiv preprint arXiv:1901.10277 (2019)
12. Lehtinen, J., et al.: Noise2Noise: learning image restoration without clean data. arXiv preprint arXiv:1803.04189 (2018)
13. Lemarchand, F., Montesuma, E.F., Pelcat, M., Nogues, E.: Opendenoising: an extensible benchmark for building comparative studies of image denoisers. arXiv preprint arXiv:1910.08328 (2019)
14. Loshchilov, I., Hutter, F.: SGDR: stochastic gradient descent with warm restarts. arXiv preprint arXiv:1608.03983 (2016)
15. Lustig, M., Donoho, D.L., Santos, J.M., Pauly, J.M.: Compressed sensing MRI. IEEE Signal Process. Mag. **25**(2), 72 (2008)
16. Mäkinen, Y., Azzari, L., Foi, A.: Exact transform-domain noise variance for collaborative filtering of stationary correlated noise. In: 2019 IEEE International Conference on Image Processing (ICIP), pp. 185–189. IEEE (2019)
17. Moran, N., Schmidt, D., Zhong, Y., Coady, P.: Noisier2Noise: learning to denoise from unpaired noisy data. In: Proceedings of the IEEE/CVF Conference on Computer Vision and Pattern Recognition, pp. 12064–12072 (2020)
18. Paszke, A., et al.: PyTorch: an imperative style, high-performance deep learning library. In: Advances in Neural Information Processing Systems, pp. 8026–8037 (2019)
19. Roberts, K., et al.: Multiplane microscopy dataset for benchmarking denoising methods (2020). https://doi.org/10.5281/zenodo.4114086

20. Ronneberger, O., Fischer, P., Brox, T.: U-Net: convolutional networks for biomedical image segmentation. In: Navab, N., Hornegger, J., Wells, W.M., Frangi, A.F. (eds.) MICCAI 2015. LNCS, vol. 9351, pp. 234–241. Springer, Cham (2015). https://doi.org/10.1007/978-3-319-24574-4_28
21. Weigert, M., et al.: Content-aware image restoration: pushing the limits of fluorescence microscopy. Nat. Methods **15**(12), 1090–1097 (2018)
22. Wu, D., Gong, K., Kim, K., Li, X., Li, Q.: Consensus neural network for medical imaging denoising with only noisy training samples. In: Shen, D., et al. (eds.) MICCAI 2019. LNCS, vol. 11767, pp. 741–749. Springer, Cham (2019). https://doi.org/10.1007/978-3-030-32251-9_81
23. Zhang, Y., et al.: A poisson-gaussian denoising dataset with real fluorescence microscopy images. In: Proceedings of the IEEE Conference on Computer Vision and Pattern Recognition, pp. 11710–11718 (2019)

Real-Time Video Denoising to Reduce Ionizing Radiation Exposure in Fluoroscopic Imaging

Dave Van Veen$^{(\boxtimes)}$, Ben A. Duffy, Long Wang, Keshav Datta, Tao Zhang, Greg Zaharchuk, and Enhao Gong

Subtle Medical Inc., Menlo Park, CA 94025, USA
{dave,ben,long,keshav,tao,greg,enhao}@subtlemedical.com

Abstract. Fluoroscopic imaging relies on ionizing radiation to provide physicians with high quality video feedback during a surgical operation. Radiation exposure is harmful for both the physician and patient, but reducing dosage results in a much noisier video. We hence propose an algorithm that delivers the same quality video with 4× reduction in radiation dose. Our method is a deep learning approximation to VBM4D, a state-of-the-art video denoiser. Neither VBM4D nor previous deep learning methods are clinically feasible, however, as their high inference runtimes prohibit live display on an operating room monitor. On the other hand, we present a video denoising method which executes orders of magnitude faster while achieving state-of-the-art performance. This provides compelling potential for real-time clinical application in fluoroscopic imaging.

Keywords: Fluoroscopic imaging · Video denoising · Real-time

1 Introduction

Image-guided surgery systems are employed by surgeons to inspect patient anatomy and guide surgical instruments during an operation. These systems provide real-time feedback of the surgeon's precise movements, which are displayed on computer monitors in the operating room. This use of imaging has become standard in many surgical operations. It enables safer and less invasive procedures as the surgeons have greater control of the procedure, hence reducing tissue trauma and disruption [27].

Due to the small size of the imaging sensor, obtaining sufficient tissue contrast for a high-quality video is difficult. To aid in this, the surgeon leverages fluoroscopy: an imaging technique in conjunction with ionizing radiation. This greatly improves image visibility on a large monitor. The downside of fluoroscopy, however, is that it requires radiation to obtain sufficient tissue contrast for a high-quality video. This radiation exposure is dangerous for both the patient and the surgeon. Patient exposure can cause DNA damage, hair loss, burns and necrosis [2]. Repetitive patient exposure has been shown to double the risk of

© Springer Nature Switzerland AG 2021
N. Haq et al. (Eds.): MLMIR 2021, LNCS 12964, pp. 109–119, 2021.
https://doi.org/10.1007/978-3-030-88552-6_11

breast cancer in women [7]. Surgeon exposure to radiation is also troubling: orthopedic surgeons are $5\times$ more likely to develop cancer in their lifetime [13]. Further, because they work with the central core of the body as opposed to extremities, spinal surgeons receive $10-12\times$ more radiation exposure compared to other orthopedic surgeons [18].

Other than protective equipment, a universally adopted technique is the principle ALARA: "As Low As Reasonably Achievable" [22]. This approach encourages the surgeon to avoid capturing an x-ray video if possible; when a video must be captured, use the lowest dose possible. Clearly there is great incentive and universal agreement to reduce exposure; however, at lower doses of radiation, the resulting video is often too noisy for clinical use.

By denoising the output videos, there is tremendous potential in providing high-quality feedback to the physician with less radiation exposure. Yet while state-of-the-art video denoising methods such as VBM4D [11] deliver excellent performance, they have very high runtime. This would introduce significant delay between video capture and subsequent display on the operating room's monitor, which is infeasible for a real-time application. We propose a method to approximate VBM4D in real-time.

1.1 Background

The problem of single-frame image denoising has been widely studied in machine learning, as convolutional neural networks (CNNs) have demonstrated exceptional performance when trained over large amounts of data [10]. Image denoising improves resolution in the spatial domain within a single frame; meanwhile, video denoising must additionally enforce temporal coherence across frames.

Video denoising is a much less studied problem. One family of solutions are patch-based algorithms: consider VBM4D [11], an extension of the popular image denoiser BM3D [4]. VBM4D constructs 3D spatiotemporal volumes by tracking blocks along motion trajectories with similar blocks, thus leveraging non-local spatial correlation as a fourth dimension. Other patch-based algorithms perform comparably to VBM4D in some cases, but they may be restricted to specific noise characteristics [21] or take several minutes to denoise a single frame [1]. The second family of solutions to video denoising consists of deep learning methods [5,12,23] such as DVDnet [24], an end-to-end trained neural network which performs spatial denoising, frame warping, and temporal denoising in subsequent steps.

The primary issue with both patch-based and deep learning methods is their reliance on an explicit stage of motion estimation/compensation. This is computationally expensive and prohibits real-time denoising capability. Recent work by Tassano et al. [25] circumvented this problem by embedding motion estimation into the network architecture itself. This achieved orders of magnitude faster runtime while maintaining similar performance to existing state-of-the-art methods. We build upon this work and demonstrate its potential for clinical application.

1.2   Our Contributions

We use deep learning to approximate state-of-the-art denoising methods, enabling orders of magnitude faster inference for real-time application. Typically, video denoising methods are demonstrated on Gaussian i.i.d. noise; however, that is not sufficient for the application of fluoroscopic imaging. Specifically we focus on spine surgery, as this is most clinically relevant due to high levels of radiation exposure [13,18]. In order to obtain training data, we first propose a novel method which simulates a low-dose video and ground truth given the original normal-dose video. We use this data to train a video denoising network with orders of magnitude faster runtime than VBM4D or other deep learning techniques. The network architecture is based on FastDVDnet [25], but we implement additional speed-up techniques to make this clinically feasible for real-time applications. We then demonstrate that, compared to the original normal-dose video, our algorithm delivers the same or better quality video with 4× reduction in radiation dose. This video comparison includes quantitative metrics and a reader study with orthopedic surgeons.

2   Methods

2.1   Data

We obtained a large dataset of 180 normal-dose fluoroscopy videos, each with varying anatomy. Video length ranges between 20−400 frames while frame size ranges from 768×768 to 1536×1536, or 0.59−2.36 megapixels (MP). This includes a combination of dynamic and static videos with frame rates between 4−30 fps. Dose level of a given video acquisition is determined by various parameters such as x-ray tube voltage, tube current, and radiation air kerma [8]. Our dataset contains videos acquired with a wide range of parameters, which we refer to as "normal dose". Low dose is defined below.

Training a deep learning model requires large amounts of paired data, which is difficult to acquire because live motion on human anatomy is not controllable. However we were able to obtain a few paired samples of normal and low dose videos on static cadavers. These paired samples were used to validate our training pair simulation procedure. We now describe this procedure (Fig. 1) in the following section.

2.2   Training Pair Simulation

Obtaining ground-truth videos with negligible amounts of noise is difficult in practice, as this would require inordinately high radiation exposure. Instead we simulate ground-truth via the following operations. Given a normal dose video, first temporally average pixels across a neighborhood of adjacent frames. This is a common denoising step performed in fluoroscopy applications [17]. For videos with motion, we limit this temporal averaging to a small neighborhood of

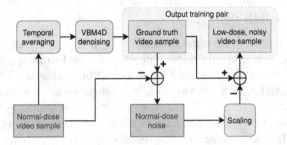

Fig. 1. Method for creation of a training pair (green) given a single normal-dose video sample as input. Scaling the normal-dose noise by a factor of c corresponds to a dose reduction of c^2 [16]. (Color figure online)

frames to avoid introducing motion blur, which would be undesirable for ground-truth data. Next we achieve spatiotemporal denoising by applying video denoiser VBM4D [11] and use the resulting output as ground-truth. All simulated ground-truth videos used in training are inspected by a surgeon to certify no artifacts have been introduced.

In order to simulate low dose videos, we first subtract the normal dose input video from ground-truth, yielding a normal dose noise map. We then scale this noise map by some constant factor c. While this constant can be arbitrarily chosen, we set $c = 2$, doubling the intensity of the noise. This corresponds to reducing the radiation dose by a factor of 4, since noise is inversely proportional to the square of radiation dose [16]. We then add this scaled noise map to the ground-truth sample, resulting in a simulation of low dose. Figure 5 in the appendix provides an example of this process and demonstrates the noise map is free from structure and artifacts.

Note that Gaussian i.i.d. is not an accurate noise model for this application [3], as we found fluoroscopy noise to be very coarse and not i.i.d. in the spatial or temporal domain. Figure 2 demonstrates the difference between fluoroscopy and Gaussian i.i.d. noise and also uses the small paired cadaver dataset to demonstrate that our simulated low-dose noise model closely matches that of of the original low-dose noise.

2.3 Denoising Model

To perform real-time video denoising, we create a variant of FastDVDnet [25], which is based off multiple modified U-net [19] blocks. Compared to other video denoisers, this algorithm forgoes the computationally expensive step of motion estimation—instead using five adjacent frames as input. Convolutional networks have shown compelling performance in solving image translation problems [26] and learning optical flow [6]. This architecture leverages these findings to handle motion by feeding multiple adjacent frames to the same U-net, hence learning motion without an explicit alignment compensation stage.

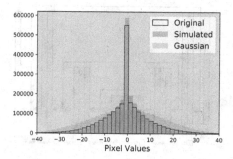 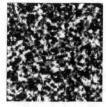 

Fig. 2. Validation of simulated fluoroscopy noise. *Left*: histogram of noise pixel values to demonstrate that the distribution of simulated noise (green) is comparable to that of the original low-dose noise (clear) and distinct from Gaussian i.i.d. noise (blue). *Middle*: single frame of fluoroscopy noise, which is very coarse and not i.i.d. in the spatial or temporal dimensions. *Right*: Single frame of Gaussian i.i.d. noise. (Color figure online)

When denoising frame f_t at time t, the input will be frames $\{f_{t-2}, f_{t-1}, f_t, ...f_{t+1}, f_{t+2}\}$, as shown in Fig. 3. Each denoising block consists of the same modified 16-layer U-net, taking as input three adjacent frames. After two steps of cascading denoising blocks, the network outputs a single denoised version of f_t, which we denote $\tilde{f}_t$. In the first step, all three denoising blocks have the same set of weights. These weights are different from those in the second step denoising block. Note that because inference only requires five frames, this method can be run in a streaming fashion throughout the video acquisition process.

We make several modifications to the original FastDVDNet to achieve real-time denoising. A simple architecture modification of combining frames in the latent space allows us to bypass the intermediate decoding step. Additionally, the output of each denoising block is cached in memory to avoid redundant computation at the next time step. Finally all floating point representations are quantized to half-precision. We notice no compromise in image quality from these modifications.

2.4   Model Training

The training data consists of pairs $\{X_t^p, \tilde{f}_t^p\}$, where $\tilde{f}_t$ is the ground-truth frame at time t, and $X_t = \{f_{t-2}, f_{t-1}, f_t, f_{t+1}, f_{t+2}\}$ is a neighborhood of five noisy, low-dose frames. The patch index p corresponds to a 256×256 patch chosen at random. The time index t corresponds to a frame chosen at random such that $2 < t \leq T - 2$, where T is the total number of frames for a given sample. The loss function for model training is $\mathcal{L}(\theta) = \mathcal{L}_1(\tilde{f}_t^p, \hat{f}_t^p) = \|\tilde{f}_t^p - \mathcal{F}(X_t^p; \theta)\|_1$, where $\hat{f}_t^p = \mathcal{F}(X_t; \theta)$ is the output of the network $\mathcal{F}$ parameterized by θ. We found that incorporating SSIM or perceptual loss into the loss function resulted in similar or worse results; hence we only use ℓ_1-loss, which provides an additional benefit of faster training time.

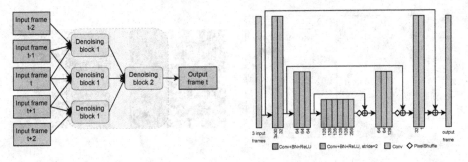

Fig. 3. *Left*: high-level structure of FastDVDnet, which inputs five consecutive frames to denoise the central frame. This network is composed of two cascading steps of denoising blocks. Each block contains the same structure, and blocks from the first step all share the same weights. *Right*: modified U-net structure of one denoising block.

3   Experiments

We now demonstrate that, with 4× lower radiation dose, our method outputs videos of equal or better quality compared to the original normal-dose videos. Furthermore we show that this can be performed in real-time, depending on frame rate and size.

This network has been implemented in PyTorch [15] with TensorRT [14]. The optimizer Adam [9] is used to minimize the loss function with learning rate 0.001 over 40 epochs with a mini-batch size of 4.

3.1   Reader Study

To obtain clinical feedback on video quality, we performed a reader study with three surgeons. Each was presented sets of two samples side-by-side in a randomized fashion: the original normal dose and our algorithm output, e.g. the second and fourth column in Fig. 4. They graded each set using a five-point Liekert scale (Table 3, appendix) on the following categories: perceived SNR, perceived resolution, overall quality, and diagnostic confidence. Our output received higher scores in each category. Please see Table 4 in the appendix for reader scores and a power analysis.

3.2   Video Quality

Metrics

To quantitatively evaluate the performance of our algorithm, we use SSIM [20], PSNR, and a time-series noise metric (TSNM) [17]. Higher values for SSIM and PSNR correspond to higher quality, which is measured in reference to ground truth. While these two metrics are commonly used to evaluate image quality,

Table 1. Video quality. In addition to outperforming VBM4D, our algorithm delivers higher quality compared to the original normal-dose video. This corresponds to a 4× reduction in radiation dose.

Metric	Low-dose (input)	Normal-dose (baseline)	Ours	VBM4D
TSNM	$1.0 \pm .45$	$0.52 \pm .25$	$\mathbf{0.29 \pm .19}$	$0.64 \pm .47$
SSIM	$0.59 \pm .14$	$0.81 \pm .10$	$\mathbf{0.86 \pm .07}$	$0.80 \pm .10$
PSNR	25.16 ± 4.10	31.40 ± 4.68	$\mathbf{32.58 \pm 4.68}$	29.18 ± 5.21

they are performed solely on a frame-by-frame basis and do not consider temporal information. As such we leverage TSNM which estimates noise in the spatiotemporal domain without relying on a ground-truth reference video. Here we normalize TSNM such that the low-dose input evaluates to 1, where lower values correspond to less noise. For example a TSNM value of 0.50 would correspond to a 2× reduction in noise compared to the low-dose input.

Results and Discussion

Our algorithm takes as input a video with 4× lower dose and produces higher video quality than the normal-dose baseline, as demonstrated in Table 1. Note that via TSNM, normal-dose videos contain roughly half the noise of low-dose videos. This aligns with our scaling the noise by a factor of $c = 2$, as discussed in Sect. 2.2.

In an effort to approximate the state-of-the-art VBM4D, our algorithm actually outperforms VBM4D on all metrics. This can be attributed to our ground-truth training data created via both VBM4D and temporal averaging. Note we do not compare against other deep learning networks for video denoising because they rely on a separate motion estimation step and are hence orders of magnitude slower [25].

Qualitative results are included in the manuscript Fig. 4 and the appendix Fig. 6. Additionally the supplemental material contains a dynamic video of a forceps being used to localize anterior cervical discectomy and fusion (ACDF), which is clinically relevant in orthopedic spine surgery.

3.3   Runtime

The viability of this video denoising method for clinical application is dependent upon runtime, as surgeons require rapid feedback in the operating room. Assuming a standard frame rate of 30 fps, real-time processing must be less than 33.3 ms/frame. Our algorithm far exceeds this in Table 2, which includes an ablation study of each individual modification we made to the original FastDVDNet, as discussed in Sect. 2.3. Note these are results on the most data-intensive case in our dataset, i.e. frame size 2.36 MP, as runtime scales linearly with number of pixels.

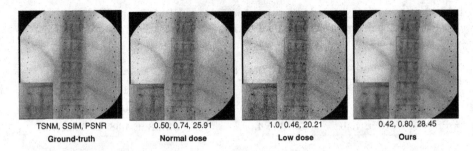

| TSNM, SSIM, PSNR | 0.50, 0.74, 25.91 | 1.0, 0.46, 20.21 | 0.42, 0.80, 28.45 |
| Ground-truth | Normal dose | Low dose | Ours |

Fig. 4. Single-frame results from a fluoroscopy video. Our model generates a single frame by taking five low-dose frames as input. Metrics are calculated with respect to ground truth. Additional results are included in the appendix and supplementary material.

Table 2. Runtime (milliseconds) for denoising a single frame with varying methods. Baseline represents the original FastDVDNet [24], while individual modifications are provided in an ablation format. Ours is a combination of each individual modification. Note that our algorithm was run on GPU, so this is not a fair comparison to VBM4D (CPU). We simply demonstrate the viability of our method for real-time clinical application, which requires a minimum of 30 fps i.e. less than 33.3 ms/frame.

Runtime (ms)	Method
109.1 ± 12.43	Baseline
78.65 ± 20.00	Baseline + architecture mod
48.14 ± 16.38	Baseline + caching
61.77 ± 5.87	Baseline + quantization
8.99 ± 5.07	**Ours** (GPU)
8786 ± 1538	VBM4D (CPU)

Recall that we do not directly compare against other deep learning techniques, as FastDVDnet is significantly faster than other networks trained on GPU [25]. While our algorithm runs on a NVIDIA Tesla V100 GPU, VBM4D is limited to an Intel i9-7920X CPU; therefore this is not a fair comparison. We merely seek to demonstrate that our method is viable for real-time clinical applications. Additionally, we note that using a NVIDIA RTX-4000 GPU resulted in 2.1× slower runtime compared to the V100.

4   Conclusion

We demonstrate clinically viable video denoising for the application of fluoroscopic imaging in spine surgery. Our methods allow for a 4× dose reduction while providing equivalent or better video quality to the normal dosage level, as supported by quantitative metrics and surgeon review. Critically, this algorithm executes in real-time. In future work we plan to pursue further clinical validation and also investigate generalization across other fluoroscopy applications.

Appendix

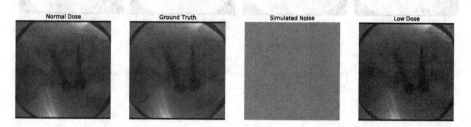

Fig. 5. Training pair simulation using the method outlined in Fig. 1, which inputs the normal dose video and outputs both a ground truth and a low dose video. We note the noise map is free of structure and artifacts.

Table 3. Five-point Liekert scale used for reader study clinical evaluation.

Score	Scoring criteria
1	The left sample is significantly superior to the right sample
2	The left sample is mildly superior to the right sample
3	Both samples are equivalent
4	The left sample is mildly inferior to the right sample
5	The left sample is significantly inferior to the right sample

Table 4. Reader study scores. Positive mean scores denote our output is superior, which holds true for each category. We use this data to create a power analysis (95% confidence, 80% power) to estimate the number of paired low/normal dose samples required for a superiority test, $n = 61$ in the worst case. While clinical acquisition was beyond the scope of this preliminary work, we plan to collect this data in the future to pursue further clinical validation.

Category	Score	n, sup.
Perceived SNR	0.83 ± 1.66	39
Perceived resolution	0.33 ± 0.84	61
Overall quality	0.5 ± 1.11	41
Diagnostic confidence	0.5 ± 1.01	39

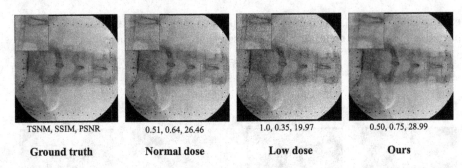

| TSNM, SSIM, PSNR | 0.51, 0.64, 26.46 | 1.0, 0.35, 19.97 | 0.50, 0.75, 28.99 |
| Ground truth | Normal dose | Low dose | Ours |

Fig. 6. Single-frame results from a fluoroscopy video. Metrics are calculated with respect to ground truth.

References

1. Arias, P., Morel, J.M.: Video denoising via empirical bayesian estimation of space-time patches. J. Math. Imag. Vis. **60**(1), 70–93 (2018)
2. Balter, S., Hopewell, J.W., Miller, D.L., Wagner, L.K., Zelefsky, M.J.: Fluoroscopically guided interventional procedures: a review of radiation effects on patients' skin and hair. Radiology **254**(2), 326–341 (2010)
3. Cesarelli, M., Bifulco, P., Cerciello, T., Romano, M., Paura, L.: X-ray fluoroscopy noise modeling for filter design. Int. J. Comput. Assist. Radiol. Surg. **8**(2), 269–278 (2013)
4. Dabov, K., Foi, A., Katkovnik, V., Egiazarian, K.: Image denoising by sparse 3-d transform-domain collaborative filtering. IEEE Trans. Image Process. **16**(8), 2080–2095 (2007)
5. Davy, A., Ehret, T., Morel, J.M., Arias, P., Facciolo, G.: Non-local video denoising by CNN. arXiv preprint arXiv:1811.12758 (2018)
6. Dosovitskiy, A., et al.: FlowNet: learning optical flow with convolutional networks. In: Proceedings of the IEEE International Conference on Computer Vision, pp. 2758–2766 (2015)
7. Hoffman, D.A., Lonstein, J.E., Morin, M.M., Visscher, W., Harris III, B.S., Boice, J.D., Jr.: Breast cancer in women with scoliosis exposed to multiple diagnostic X rays. JNCI J. Natl. Cancer Inst. **81**(17), 1307–1312 (1989)
8. Huda, W.: Kerma-area product in diagnostic radiology. Am. J. Roentgenol. **203**(6), W565–W569 (2014)
9. Kingma, D.P., Ba, J.: Adam: a method for stochastic optimization. arXiv preprint arXiv:1412.6980 (2014)
10. Krizhevsky, A., Sutskever, I., Hinton, G.E.: ImageNet classification with deep convolutional neural networks. In: Advances in Neural Information Processing Systems, pp. 1097–1105 (2012)
11. Maggioni, M., Boracchi, G., Foi, A., Egiazarian, K.: Video denoising, deblocking, and enhancement through separable 4-d nonlocal spatiotemporal transforms. IEEE Trans. Image Process. **21**(9), 3952–3966 (2012)
12. Maggioni, M., Huang, Y., Li, C., Xiao, S., Fu, Z., Song, F.: Efficient multi-stage video denoising with recurrent spatio-temporal fusion. arXiv preprint arXiv:2103.05407 (2021)

13. Mastrangelo, G., Fedeli, U., Fadda, E., Giovanazzi, A., Scoizzato, L., Saia, B.: Increased cancer risk among surgeons in an orthopaedic hospital. Occup. Med. **55**(6), 498–500 (2005)

14. NVIDIA: Tensorrt open source software (2018). https://developer.nvidia.com/tensorrt

15. Paszke, A., et al.: Automatic differentiation in PyTorch (2017)

16. Primak, A.N., McCollough, C.H., Bruesewitz, M.R., Zhang, J., Fletcher, J.G.: Relationship between noise, dose, and pitch in cardiac multi-detector row CT. Radiographics **26**(6), 1785–1794 (2006)

17. Prince, J.L., Links, J.M.: Medical Imaging Signals and Systems. Pearson Prentice Hall, Upper Saddle River (2006)

18. Rampersaud, Y.R., Foley, K.T., Shen, A.C., Williams, S., Solomito, M.: Radiation exposure to the spine surgeon during fluoroscopically assisted pedicle screw insertion. Spine **25**(20), 2637–2645 (2000)

19. Ronneberger, O., Fischer, P., Brox, T.: U-Net: convolutional networks for biomedical image segmentation. In: Navab, N., Hornegger, J., Wells, W.M., Frangi, A.F. (eds.) MICCAI 2015. LNCS, vol. 9351, pp. 234–241. Springer, Cham (2015). https://doi.org/10.1007/978-3-319-24574-4_28

20. Sampat, M.P., Wang, Z., Gupta, S., Bovik, A.C., Markey, M.K.: Complex wavelet structural similarity: a new image similarity index. IEEE Trans. Image Process. **18**(11), 2385–2401 (2009)

21. Sarno, A., et al.: Real-time algorithm for poissonian noise reduction in low-dose fluoroscopy: performance evaluation. Biomed. Eng. Online **18**(1), 1–21 (2019)

22. Slovis, T.L.: Children, computed tomography radiation dose, and the as low as reasonably achievable (ALARA) concept. Pediatrics **112**(4), 971–972 (2003)

23. Tang, X., Zhen, P., Kang, M., Yi, H., Wang, W., Chen, H.B.: Learning enriched features for video denoising with convolutional neural network. In: 2020 IEEE Asia Pacific Conference on Circuits and Systems (APCCAS), pp. 248–251. IEEE (2020)

24. Tassano, M., Delon, J., Veit, T.: DVDNet: a fast network for deep video denoising. In: 2019 IEEE International Conference on Image Processing (ICIP), pp. 1805–1809. IEEE (2019)

25. Tassano, M., Delon, J., Veit, T.: FastDVDNet: towards real-time deep video denoising without flow estimation. In: Proceedings of the IEEE/CVF Conference on Computer Vision and Pattern Recognition, pp. 1354–1363 (2020)

26. Wu, S., Xu, J., Tai, Y.-W., Tang, C.-K.: Deep high dynamic range imaging with large foreground motions. In: Ferrari, V., Hebert, M., Sminchisescu, C., Weiss, Y. (eds.) ECCV 2018. LNCS, vol. 11206, pp. 120–135. Springer, Cham (2018). https://doi.org/10.1007/978-3-030-01216-8_8

27. Zhou, K.-H., Luo, C.-F., Chen, N., Hu, C.-F., Pan, F.-G.: Minimally invasive surgery under fluoro-navigation for anterior pelvic ring fractures. Indian J. Orthopaedics **50**(3), 250–255 (2016). https://doi.org/10.4103/0019-5413.181791

A Frequency Domain Constraint for Synthetic and Real X-ray Image Super Resolution

Qing Ma[1(✉)], Jae Chul Koh[2], and WonSook Lee[1]

[1] University of Ottawa, Ottawa, Canada
{qma088,wslee}@uottawa.ca
[2] Korea University Anam Hospital, Seoul, Korea

Abstract. Synthetic X-ray images are simulated X-ray images projected from CT data. High-quality synthetic X-ray images can facilitate various applications such as surgical image guidance systems and VR training simulations. However, it is difficult to produce high-quality arbitrary view synthetic X-ray images in real-time due to different CT slice thickness, high computational cost, and the complexity of algorithms. Our goal is to generate high-resolution synthetic X-ray images in real-time by upsampling low-resolution images with deep learning-based super-resolution methods. Reference-based Super Resolution (RefSR) has been well studied in recent years and has shown higher performance than traditional Single Image Super-Resolution (SISR). It can produce fine details by utilizing the reference image but still inevitably generates some artifacts and noise. In this paper, we introduce frequency domain loss as a constraint to further improve the quality of the RefSR results with fine details and without obvious artifacts. To the best of our knowledge, this is the first paper utilizing the frequency domain for the loss functions in the field of super-resolution. We achieved good results in evaluating our method on both synthetic and real X-ray image datasets.

Keywords: Synthetic X-ray · Super resolution · Frequency domain · Digital reconstructed radiographs

1 Introduction

Efforts have been made on converting CT volume or slice images into synthetic X-ray images, also known as Digital Reconstructed Radiographs (DRRs), with fast rendering algorithms such as ray tracing or ray casting methods [1–4]. In recent years, deep learning aided algorithms can generate highly realistic X-ray images but require vast training data and high computation resources [5, 6]. In general, there are three challenges to high-quality synthetic X-ray image generation. Firstly, it demands high computation resources to produce high-quality synthetic X-ray images, preventing the use in clinics or hospitals. Secondly, the algorithms for generating high-quality synthetic X-ray images are often time-consuming or complex. Finally, the thickness of the scan is not thin enough due to high dose radiation of CT scanning. The gaps between slices yield lower resolution in certain views. A basic requirement for generating fine synthetic X-ray images is that the

© Springer Nature Switzerland AG 2021
N. Haq et al. (Eds.): MLMIR 2021, LNCS 12964, pp. 120–129, 2021.
https://doi.org/10.1007/978-3-030-88552-6_12

resolution is approximately equal in all views [7]. Thus, it is necessary to up-sample the lower resolution views, either with interpolation or more sophisticated methods such as semantic interpolation [8] or super-resolution (SR) methods.

Various application scenarios have been explored with synthetic X-ray images. For example, synthetic X-ray images are used in virtual reality (VR) training simulation for training physicians on fluoroscopy-guided intervention procedures [9, 10]. It intends to replace real-life training sessions which are costly and exposed to radiation. High-quality DDRs can also be used to train deep learning models for diagnostic tasks [5]. It's also been found that using synthetic X-ray images can reduce up to half the amount of fluoroscopic images taken during real fluoroscopy-guided intervention procedures [11]. The performance of the above applications could all benefit from higher-quality synthetic X-ray image data sources.

Deep learning-based SR methods have been well explored for natural images. There are two main categories which are Single Image Super-Resolution (SISR) and Reference-based super-resolution (RefSR). SISR aims to reconstruct a high-resolution (HR) image from a single low-resolution (LR) image [12]. RefSR works on learning finer texture details from a given reference HR image [13]. Convolution neural networks (CNN) and Generative adversarial network (GAN) methods have been widely used in SISR. CNN models can reach high performance on evaluation metrics but produce overly smooth images with coarse details. On the other hand, GAN models generate appealing images with fine details but with more artifacts. This issue is especially crucial in medical imaging as image details have an impact on diagnosis and decision-making during operations. RefSR can learn fine texture details from the reference image but still generate some artifacts and noise. Fourier transform is rarely utilized in the field of super-resolution. We propose to use a frequency domain loss as a constraint to mitigate this problem.

We used a matrix-based projection algorithm and custom-built lookup tables created with tissue radiographic opacity parameters to generate fine LR synthetic X-ray images from CT slices in arbitrary views. And then, we use a RefSR method combined with our frequency domain loss to generate HR synthetic X-ray images with few artifacts and noise. We achieved good results on both synthetic and real X-ray image super-resolution with our proposed TTSR-FD.

2   Related Work

Deep learning was first used in SISR by Dong et al. [14]. They proposed SRCNN achieved superior results compared to previous conventional SR methods. Lim et al. [12] proposed EDSR introduced Residual Block into SISR that further boosts the model performance. Zhang et al. [15] added the attention mechanism to improve the network performance. These methods used CNN yield a strong PSNR performance. However, the results do not have a good visual quality for human perceptions. GAN gradually become successful in the field known for good visual quality. Ledig et al. [16] proposed SRGAN first adopted GAN and showed appealing image quality. Wang et al. [17] introduced Residual-in-Residual Dense Block and relativistic GAN further improved the perceptual quality of the results.

RefSR takes advantage of learning more accurate texture details from the HR reference image. The reference image could be selected from adjacent frames in a video, images from different viewpoints, etc. [18]. It can achieve visually appealing results without generating many artifacts and noise compared to GAN-based SISR. Zheng et al. [19] proposed CrossNet that adopted a flow-based cross-scale warping to transfer features. SRNTT [18] adopted patch matching with VGG extracted features and can use arbitrary images as references. Yang et al. [13] proposed TTSR applied a transformer network with attention models that outperformed traditional SISR methods. Nevertheless, these models still generate perceivable artifacts and noise in the resulting image.

Fourier transform is a powerful tool in the field of signal processing, and it has also shown great potential in deep learning-related research. Souza and Frayne [20] proposed a hybrid framework for magnetic resonance (MR) image reconstruction that learns in both frequency and spatial domain. Li et al. [21] proposed the first neural network SR method by solely learning in the frequency domain. It shows advantages on the speed of the model but with an imperceptible loss on the quality of results. Xu et al. [22] proposed a novel learning-based frequency channel selection method that achieved superior results on multiple tasks. In this work, we introduce to compute a loss function in frequency domain as a constraint for the neural network, instead of transferring the network itself into frequency domain.

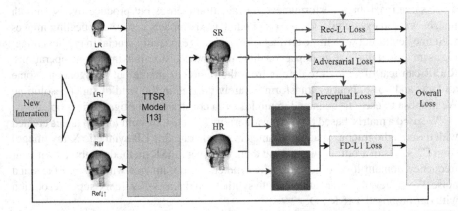

Fig. 1. Overview of our TTSR-FD method. We add the frequency domain loss on the TTSR [13] model. The four input images are LR, up-sampled LR, reference images (Ref) and down/up-sampled Ref Image. These rescaling operations will help to improve the texture transfer accuracy [13]. SR image is the model output. HR image is the ground truth image.

3 Methods

We aim to reduce the artifacts generated by the network while not losing fine details. To achieve this, we made a thoughtful analysis in the frequency domain for SR methods and introduce frequency domain loss with TTSR [13] as illustrated in Fig. 1. We first explore the frequency domain pattern for images of different quality. Then, we introduce our loss function computed in the frequency domain.

3.1 Frequency Domain Analysis

We adopt Fourier transform to reveal frequency patterns that are not visible in the spatial domain. Different image samples are shown in both spatial and frequency domain in Fig. 2. While the bicubic interpolated image shows the worst results, we observe high-frequency details are also not fully learned by any of the SR models. We show our TTSR-FD result as a comparison of the improvement.

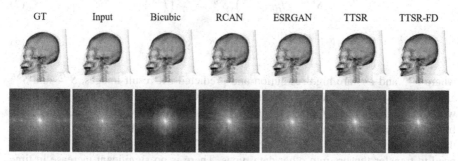

Fig. 2. Images in the both spatial and frequency domain from left to right are ground truth, LR input, Bicubic upsampling, and RCAN, ESRGAN, TTSR, TTSR-FD SR methods results.

In general, we can see whiter regions in the center indicating images contain more low-frequency content. The input image loses lots of high-frequency details compare to the GT. The bicubic upsampling is not able to produce any high-frequency details. Limited high-frequency details are generated by RCAN. ESRGAN can learn some good high-frequency details and shows sharp details in the spatial domain. But we can see abnormal patterns in frequency domain such as a rectangle shape contour in the center. This indicates it generates artifacts to satisfy human perceptual. TTSR can generate fine high-frequency details but also fails to match some patterns. Our TTSR-FD got the best similarity in frequency domain compared to GT. We can find out that the frequency domain contains lots of information that is not shown in the spatial domain.

3.2 Frequency Domain Loss

We make a hypothesis based on the observation from the previous section that a loss function computed in the frequency domain can increase the resulting image quality of RefSR. We aim to use this loss to set up a constraint during training that can force the model to learn more from the data and generate fewer artifacts and noise. We choose to build it with a pixel-wise loss function to ensure the network learns from the frequency domain patterns. We utilize $L1$ loss which is proven effective for SR methods, also more robust and easier to converge compared to $L2$ loss. Our network architecture is shown in Fig. 1. In short, we compute the loss by transferring model output and ground truth images of each iteration into frequency domain, calculate their $L1$ loss and feed back to the network. We applied this loss to our baseline model TTSR [13], which has three loss functions. The overall loss of our TTSR-FD model is:

$$\mathcal{L}_{overall} = \lambda_{rec}\mathcal{L}_{rec} + \lambda_{fd}\mathcal{L}_{fd} + \lambda_{adv}\mathcal{L}_{adv} + \lambda_{per}\mathcal{L}_{per} \qquad (1)$$

where $\mathcal{L}_{rec}$ is the reconstruction loss with $L1$ loss. $\mathcal{L}_{adv}$ is the adversarial loss using WGAN-GP [23]. $\mathcal{L}_{per}$ is the perceptual loss that include a normal perceptual loss and a texture wise loss [13]. We added a frequency domain loss $\mathcal{L}_{fd}$ to improve the network performance. λ is the weight coefficients for the loss functions that are optimized through vast expiriments. In each iteration, a batch of SR and HR images are transferred into the frequency domain and then calculated their $L1$ loss.

$$S^{HR} = f_{rfft}\left(I^{HR}\right), S^{SR} = f_{rfft}\left(I^{SR}\right) \tag{2}$$

$$\mathcal{L}_{fd} = \frac{1}{CHW}||S^{HR} - S^{SR}||_1 \tag{3}$$

where I^{HR} and I^{SR} are high resolution and predicted SR result images. S^{HR} and S^{SR} are the corresponding frequency domain images. C, H, W are the channel, height and width of the HR image. f_{rfft} represent the real-to-complex discrete Fourier transform function. We adopt real-to-complex discrete Fourier transform from Pytorch to improve the computation efficiency. We use the built-in FFT function from PyTorch without the need to transfer tensors into other data types. There is no significant increase in time complexity when using our frequency domain loss during training.

4 Experiments

4.1 Dataset

We create two reference-based SR datasets to evaluate our method, a synthetic head X-ray images dataset and a real chest X-ray images dataset. Both datasets are constructed following similar approaches described in [18] while making some adjustments considering the characteristic of synthetic and real X-ray images.

The synthetic X-ray images dataset is created from head CT data provided by Korea University Anam Hospital. It contains seven different head CT series from five patients with Sagittal (SAG) and Coronal (COR) views. The number of slices in these series ranges from 48 to 145 and each slice resolution is 512×512. We used different linear interpolation variables to fill the gaps between slices for each series. Our projection method is developed in Python with Numba. In the training set, we use a sampling step of $24°$ for both x and y-axis to generate 225 (15×15) input images for each CT series. The corresponding reference image is generated with a random projection angle range from $-45°$ to $45°$. The training images are then cropped into five patches of 160×160 for each input image and reference image. The LR images are generated by downsampling the input images. We build a small and large training set SynXray_S and SynXray_L. Each of them consists of 410 and 1350 image pairs. We choose to leave at least one patient out during training to make sure our test data is not seen during training. The test set images are generated with a sampling step of $20°$. There are 30 image groups in the test set from all five patients.

We also create a real chest X-ray images dataset (ChestXrayRef) from ChestX-ray8 [24] dataset for RefSR. We construct the dataset using a similar method in [18]. However, the ChestX-ray8 dataset only has X-ray images in a single frontal view. This makes it impossible to construct the dataset like synthetic X-ray images where the reference image is from a different viewpoint. We choose to randomly pick another chest X-ray image from the dataset as the reference image. This will certainly weaken the ability of RefSR method to reconstruct high-resolution textures, but it is also proven that the reference image doesn't have to be related to the input image [18]. All images are randomly picked and resized to 512×512 resolution. The training data has 1298 image pairs. The testing set has 23 image groups.

4.2 Training Details

We used a similar training parameter setting as in TTSR [13]. We use Pytorch 1.81 to implement our network. We trained 100 epochs and pick the highest performance model for all datasets. We applied the same parameter setting in all our training. We use a batch size of 4. The learning rate is 1e−4 and Adam optimizer with $\beta_1 = 0.9$, $\beta_2 = 0.999$ and $\epsilon = 1e-8$. The weight coefficient of the frequency domain loss is 1e−2. The weight coefficient for $\mathcal{L}_{rec}$, $\mathcal{L}_{adv}$, $\mathcal{L}_{per}$ are 1, 1e−3 and 1e−2, respectively. We trained our network for a scaling factor of x4. We use bicubic kernel for rescaling the input and reference images. We trained our model with a Tesla P100 GPU. The training time for large and small synthetic datasets is around 10 and 4 h respectively. The training time for the real X-ray dataset is around 18 h.

4.3 Results

We first compare our method on synthetic X-ray images dataset with state-of-the-art methods, such as RCAN [15], ESRGAN [17] and TTSR [13]. We make some modifications to our baseline model TTSR for training grayscale images, where we duplicate the grayscale channel into three channels corresponds to RGB channels for natural images then feed to the neural network. We retrain RCAN and ESRGAN models on the paired SISR dataset version of our dataset for comparison purposes as well. We evaluate our method on PSNR and SSIM as shown in Table 1. TTSR-FD achieves superior performance on both metrics. We also observe that TTSR-FD is strong on learning from a small dataset which indicates it can learn more from the data. This can be beneficial for real-life applications since medical data are hard to obtain.

We show the visual comparison for our method trained with SynXray_S on the test set in Fig. 3, consider that the visual difference between large and small datasets is minimal for our method. RCAN shows the second-highest accuracy in the quantitative measurement but we observe the image is overly smoothed and has limited high-frequency details. We can observe that the noise from the red circle area and black dots artifacts from the red rectangle area in TTSR have been removed in TTSR-FD. Our method can generate fine details without generating much noise and artifacts.

Table 1. PSNR/SSIM comparison among different SR methods on SynXray_S and SynXray_L datasets. The best results are in bold.

Method	SynXray_S	SynXray_L
RCAN	38.597/0.9482	38.880/0.9496
ESRGAN	34.483/0.9023	35.270/0.9140
TTSR	37.953/0.9393	38.115/0.9431
TTSR-FD (ours)	**39.009/0.9521**	**39.261/ 0.9514**

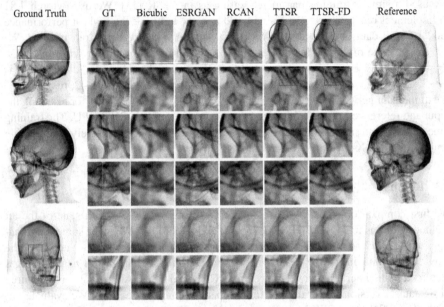

Fig. 3. Visual comparison for our method on the testing set. Example input and Ref images are generated from CT series in sagittal (1, 2) and coronal (3) view. TTSR-FD is ours.

We further test our model on Real chest X-ray images. The two models have similar quantitative results as shown in Table 2. However, we find out that the artifacts generated in TTSR-FD are significantly less than in TTSR results as shown in Fig. 4. This validates the effectiveness and generalizability of our proposed method.

Table 2. PSNR/SSIM comparison among TTSR and TTSR-FD on ChestXrayRef dataset

Method	PSNR	SSIM
TTSR	**36.767**	0.9457
TTSR-FD	36.766	**0.9470**

4.4 Ablation Study

In this section, we further verify the effectiveness of our proposed method. We set up TTSR-Rec101 that has the same ratio of weight coefficients distribution as TTSR-FD where we only increase the weight coefficients of reconstruction loss $\mathcal{L}_{rec}$ from 1 to 1.01, compared to the weight coefficients of TTSR-FD for $\mathcal{L}_{rec}$ and $\mathcal{L}_{fd}$ are 1 and 0.01. The weight coefficients of other loss functions are the same for both models. Our results are shown in Table 3. The proposed frequency domain loss significantly improved the model performance. We show the resulting images in frequency domain in Fig. 5. We can see that without frequency domain loss, increasing the weight coefficient of the reconstruction loss could not improve the similarity of high-frequency patterns in frequency domain. We observe that the vertical line patterns are not learned by TTSR-rec101 or TTSR as shown in red arrows.

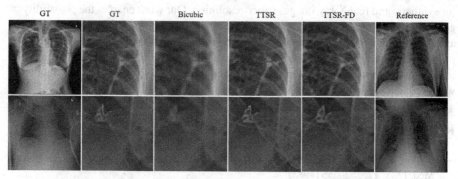

Fig. 4. Real chest X-ray visual comparison between TTSR and TTSR-FD

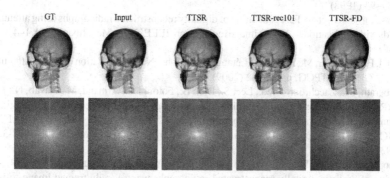

Fig. 5. Ablation study on frequency domain loss. Vertical line patterns indicated in red arrows in the ground truth image are only learned by TTSR-FD.

Table 3. Ablation study for frequency domain loss with SynXray_S dataset

Method	PSNR	SSIM
TTSR	37.953	0.9393
TTSR-Rec101	38.245	0.9405
TTSR-FD	**39.009**	**0.9521**

5 Conclusion

We proposed a texture transformer super-resolution with frequency domain loss as a constraint for synthetic and real X-ray image super-resolution. We demonstrate that an additional loss function computed in the frequency domain can improve the image quality for synthetic and real X-ray images super-resolution. Our work enables the possibility of generating high-quality synthetic X-ray images in real-time for image guiding systems and VR simulations. Even though the experiments were done on X-ray images, the proposed method is applicable for other medical images. In future works, we would like to explore more possible loss variants and other application scenarios such as denoising with frequency domain loss.

References

1. Siddon, R.L.: Fast calculation of the exact radiological path for a three-dimensional CT array. Med. Phys. **12**, 252–255 (1985)
2. Jacobs, F., Sundermann, E., De Sutter, B., Christiaens, M., Lemahieu, I.: A fast algorithm to calculate the exact radiological path through a pixel or voxel space. J. Comput. Inf. Technol. **6**, 89–94 (1998)
3. Russakoff, D.B., et al.: Fast generation of digitally reconstructed radiographs using attenuation fields with application to 2D-3D image registration. IEEE Trans. Med. Imaging **24**, 1441–1454 (2005)
4. Vidal, F.P., Garnier, M., Freud, N., Létang, J.-M., John, N.W.: Simulation of X-ray Attenuation on the GPU. In: TPCG, pp. 25–32 (2009)
5. Unberath, M., Zaech, Jan-Nico., Lee, S., Bier, B., Fotouhi, J., Armand, M., Navab, N.: Deep-DRR – a catalyst for machine learning in fluoroscopy-guided procedures. In: Frangi, A.F., Schnabel, J.A., Davatzikos, C., Alberola-López, C., Fichtinger, G. (eds.) MICCAI 2018. LNCS, vol. 11073, pp. 98–106. Springer, Cham (2018). https://doi.org/10.1007/978-3-030-00937-3_12
6. Dhont, J., Verellen, D., Mollaert, I., Vanreusel, V., Vandemeulebroucke, J.: RealDRR–rendering of realistic digitally reconstructed radiographs using locally trained image-to-image translation. Radiother. Oncol. **153**, 213–219 (2020)
7. Lin, E., Alessio, A.: What are the basic concepts of temporal, contrast, and spatial resolution in cardiac CT? J. Cardiovasc. Comput. Tomogr. **3**, 403–408 (2009). https://doi.org/10.1016/j.jcct.2009.07.003
8. Li, J., Koh, J.C., Lee, W.-S.: HRINet: alternative supervision network for high-resolution CT image interpolation. In: 2020 IEEE International Conference on Image Processing (ICIP), pp. 1916–1920 (2020). https://doi.org/10.1109/ICIP40778.2020.9191060
9. Allen, D.R.: Simulation Approaches to X-ray C-Arm-based Interventions 85

10. Korzeniowski, P., White, R.J., Bello, F.: VCSim3: a VR simulator for cardiovascular interventions. Int. J. Comput. Assist. Radiol. Surg. **13**(1), 135–149 (2017). https://doi.org/10.1007/s11548-017-1679-1

11. Touchette, M., et al.: The effect of artificial X-rays on C-arm positioning performance in a simulated orthopaedic surgical setting. Int. J. Comput. Assist. Radiol. Surg. **16**(1), 11–22 (2020). https://doi.org/10.1007/s11548-020-02280-2

12. Lim, B., Son, S., Kim, H., Nah, S., Mu Lee, K.: Enhanced deep residual networks for single image super-resolution. In: Proceedings of the IEEE Conference on Computer Vision and Pattern Recognition Workshops, pp. 136–144 (2017)

13. Yang, F., Yang, H., Fu, J., Lu, H., Guo, B.: Learning texture transformer network for image super-resolution. arXiv:2006.04139 [cs] (2020)

14. Dong, C., Loy, C.C., He, K., Tang, X.: Image super-resolution using deep convolutional networks. IEEE Trans. Pattern Anal. Mach. Intell. **38**, 295–307 (2015)

15. Zhang, Y., Li, K., Li, K., Wang, L., Zhong, B., Fu, Y.: Image super-resolution using very deep residual channel attention networks. In: Ferrari, V., Hebert, M., Sminchisescu, C., Weiss, Y. (eds.) ECCV 2018. LNCS, vol. 11211, pp. 294–310. Springer, Cham (2018). https://doi.org/10.1007/978-3-030-01234-2_18

16. Ledig, C., et al.: Photo-realistic single image super-resolution using a generative adversarial network. In: Proceedings of the IEEE Conference on Computer Vision and Pattern Recognition, pp. 4681–4690 (2017)

17. Wang, X., et al.: ESRGAN: enhanced super-resolution generative adversarial networks. In: Leal-Taixé, L., Roth, S. (eds.) ECCV 2018. LNCS, vol. 11133, pp. 63–79. Springer, Cham (2019). https://doi.org/10.1007/978-3-030-11021-5_5

18. Zhang, Z., Wang, Z., Lin, Z., Qi, H.: Image super-resolution by neural texture transfer. In: Proceedings of the IEEE/CVF Conference on Computer Vision and Pattern Recognition, pp. 7982–7991 (2019)

19. Zheng, H., Ji, M., Wang, H., Liu, Y., Fang, L.: CrossNet: an end-to-end reference-based super resolution network using cross-scale warping. In: Ferrari, V., Hebert, M., Sminchisescu, C., Weiss, Y. (eds.) ECCV 2018. LNCS, vol. 11210, pp. 87–104. Springer, Cham (2018). https://doi.org/10.1007/978-3-030-01231-1_6

20. Souza, R., Frayne, R.: A hybrid frequency-domain/image-domain deep network for magnetic resonance image reconstruction. In: 2019 32nd SIBGRAPI Conference on Graphics, Patterns and Images (SIBGRAPI), pp. 257–264 (2019). https://doi.org/10.1109/SIBGRAPI.2019.00042.

21. Li, J., You, S., Robles-Kelly, A.: A frequency domain neural network for fast image super-resolution. In: 2018 International Joint Conference on Neural Networks (IJCNN), pp. 1–8. IEEE (2018)

22. Xu, K., Qin, M., Sun, F., Wang, Y., Chen, Y.-K., Ren, F.: Learning in the frequency domain. In: Proceedings of the IEEE/CVF Conference on Computer Vision and Pattern Recognition, pp. 1740–1749 (2020)

23. Gulrajani, I., Ahmed, F., Arjovsky, M., Dumoulin, V., Courville, A.: Improved training of wasserstein gans. arXiv preprint arXiv:1704.00028 (2017)

24. Wang, X., Peng, Y., Lu, L., Lu, Z., Bagheri, M., Summers, R.M.: ChestX-Ray8: hospital-scale chest X-ray database and benchmarks on weakly-supervised classification and localization of common thorax diseases. In: 2017 IEEE Conference on Computer Vision and Pattern Recognition (CVPR), pp. 3462–3471 (2017). https://doi.org/10.1109/CVPR.2017.369

Semi- and Self-supervised Multi-view Fusion of 3D Microscopy Images Using Generative Adversarial Networks

Canyu Yang, Dennis Eschweiler[iD], and Johannes Stegmaier[✉][iD]

Institute of Imaging and Computer Vision, RWTH Aachen University,
Aachen, Germany
johannes.stegmaier@lfb.rwth-aachen.de

Abstract. Recent developments in fluorescence microscopy allow capturing high-resolution 3D images over time for living model organisms. To be able to image even large specimens, techniques like multi-view light-sheet imaging record different orientations at each time point that can then be fused into a single high-quality volume. Based on measured point spread functions (PSF), deconvolution and content fusion are able to largely revert the inevitable degradation occurring during the imaging process. Classical multi-view deconvolution and fusion methods mainly use iterative procedures and content-based averaging. Lately, Convolutional Neural Networks (CNNs) have been deployed to approach 3D single-view deconvolution microscopy, but the multi-view case waits to be studied. We investigated the efficacy of CNN-based multi-view deconvolution and fusion with two synthetic data sets that mimic developing embryos and involve either two or four complementary 3D views. Compared with classical state-of-the-art methods, the proposed semi- and self-supervised models achieve competitive and superior deconvolution and fusion quality in the two-view and quad-view cases, respectively.

Keywords: Multi-view fusion · Convolutional Neural Networks ·
Image deconvolution · Multi-view light-sheet microscopy

1 Introduction

The life science community has put forward increasing efforts in 3D+t microscopy imaging to enable detailed recordings of biological activity in living model organisms such as gene expression patterns, tissue formation and cell differentiation [2,4,7]. Fluorescence microscopy as the most commonly used technique for observing live embryos has been facing limitations summarized by the design-space tetrahedron: resolution, speed, phototoxicity and imaging depth [27]. Light-sheet microscopy achieves real-time imaging speed and lessens phototoxicity using thin optical sectioning [2,4]. By recording the same specimen

This work was funded by the German Research Foundation DFG with the grant STE2802/2-1 (DE).

© Springer Nature Switzerland AG 2021
N. Haq et al. (Eds.): MLMIR 2021, LNCS 12964, pp. 130–139, 2021.
https://doi.org/10.1007/978-3-030-88552-6_13

from multiple orientations, *e.g.*, with multi-view light-sheet microscopy [2,7], even larger specimens can be imaged at high spatial resolution. Subsequently, multi-view fusion techniques can be used to merge the best-quality image content from all input views into a consistently sharp fusion volume [15]. Compared with content-based multi-view fusion [15], multi-view deconvolution essentially performs fusion of deconvolved views and thus results in sharper images [14].

Inspired by the CycleGAN-based 3D single-view deconvolution microscopy by Lim *et al.* [9,10], we extend their approach to 3D multi-view deconvolution and fusion using semi- and self-supervised network architectures and PSFs measured from experiments [14]. Compared with the state-of-the-art method EBMD [14], the proposed models achieve comparable and superior deconvolution and fusion quality on a set of synthetic two-view and quad-view data sets, respectively.

2 Related Work

Deep learning has been extensively exploited to resolve single-view deblurring and deconvolution for 2D natural images [8,19–21,24,25,28,29]. Regarding 3D fluorescence microscopy images, Weigert *et al.* investigated and proved the efficacy of deep learning in single-view deconvolution using 2D slices [27]. Lim *et al.* introduced the CycleGAN architecture to 3D blind deconvolution microscopy using unpaired ground-truth images that were obtained with classical methods to regularize the image style of fusion volumes [10,30]. This semi-supervised model was further adapted to non-blind deconvolution by Lim *et al.* such that known PSFs can be explicitly implemented [9]. To our best knowledge, deep learning has not been introduced to multi-view deconvolution and fusion for 3D microscopy images yet, while traditional methods have delivered reasonable performance. For instance, Verneer *et al.* designed an optimization-based deconvolution algorithm for light-sheet microscopy images that minimizes the difference between degraded fusion volume and input views using maximum *a posteriori* estimation with Gaussian noise (MAPG) [23]. Preibisch *et al.* proposed content-based image fusion (CBIF) where the fusion volume is computed as the entropy-weighted average of all input views [15]. In 2014, Preibisch *et al.* adapted the Richardson-Lucy deconvolution algorithm [12,17] to multi-view geometry and derived more efficient update schemes [14]. This algorithm named Efficient Bayesian-based Multi-view Deconvolution (EBMD) achieved the state-of-the-art fusion quality compared with CBIF [15] and MAPG [23] and will serve as the baseline for benchmarking our learning-based pipelines for multi-view deconvolution and fusion that are presented in the next section.

3 Methods

The image formation process in fluorescence microscopy can be considered as a latent image with an unknown distribution of fluorescence emitted from the specimen that is imaged through the microscope, producing a blurry image [3]. Following the notation in [9,10], we refer to the degraded image domain as $\mathcal{X}$

and the latent image domain as $\mathcal{Z}$. The imaging system can be modeled as the convolution of the latent image $z \in \mathcal{Z}$ with the respective PSF h, *i.e.*, $s = z * h$, where $*$ denotes convolution operation. An observed image $x \in \mathcal{X}$ results from the signal s being corrupted by noise n and can be modeled as:

$$x = z * h + n. \tag{1}$$

Image deconvolution is an ill-posed inverse problem as an observed image x can result from numerous plausible explanations in the latent image domain $\mathcal{Z}$. In the multi-view case, the inverse problem is formulated for each view, making the restoration of the true latent image even more difficult. Our proposed semi- and self-supervised pipelines are shown in Fig. 1.

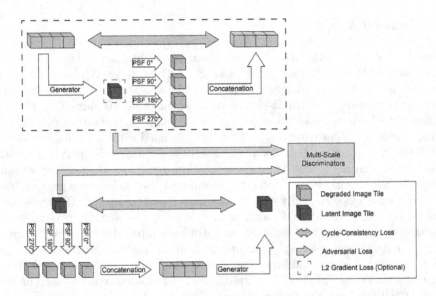

Fig. 1. Semi- and self-supervised quad-view deconvolution and fusion pipeline. Top: generator fuses four raw input views into a sharp latent image (multi-view imaging around y-axis). The generated latent image is then blurred by four known PSFs to reproduce the four degraded raw input views. Bottom: a deconvolved ground truth image is transformed to four raw image views using the known PSFs and the generator is again used to reconstruct the deconvolved ground truth image. The loss function involves an adversarial loss with multi-scale discriminators to encourage the generator to produce realistic deconvolution results and an additional cycle consistency loss in both paths to restrict the target distribution so that the generated latent image can reproduce the input views through degradation. The self-supervised network does not involve known ground truth and features only the cycle-consistency loss and an L2 gradient loss, *i.e.*, the variant involves only the part indicated by the dashed rectangle.

The generator G_Θ maps a degraded image x to a noise-free sharp image z. The discriminator D_Φ distinguishes the generated sharp image $G_\Theta(x)$ from true latent images z. Considering non-blind deconvolution, the generator modeling the degradation process $\mathcal{Z} \to \mathcal{X}$ can be defined as a convolution with PSF h. Consequently, the corresponding discriminator can be omitted to improve training efficiency. Least Squares GAN (LS-GAN) loss [13] is adopted to minimize the adversarial loss with respect to the model parameters Φ and Θ as follows:

$$\min_\Phi \frac{1}{2}\mathbb{E}_{z \sim p_z(z)}[(D_\Phi(z) - 1)^2] + \frac{1}{2}\mathbb{E}_{x \sim p_x(x)}[D_\Phi(G_\Theta(x))^2] \tag{2}$$

$$\min_\Theta \mathbb{E}_{x \sim p_x(x)}[(D_\Phi(G_\Theta(x)) - 1)^2], \tag{3}$$

where $p_x(x)$ is the distribution of degraded image x, and $p_z(z)$ is distribution of true latent image. In line with [9], we found that the LS-GAN loss provided the most stable training convergence. The cycle consistency proposed in [30] is imposed in both cycles, i.e., $\mathcal{X} \to \mathcal{Z} \to \mathcal{X}$ and $\mathcal{Z} \to \mathcal{X} \to \mathcal{Z}$, for the purpose of enforcing the generator to predict latent images in conformity with the view image formation defined in Eq. (1). The cycle consistency loss is minimized in an $L1$ sense such that:

$$L_{cycle}(\Theta) = \mathbb{E}_{x \sim p_x(x)}[\|G_\Theta(x) * h - x\|_1] + \mathbb{E}_{z \sim p_z(z)}[\|G_\Theta(z * h) - z\|_1]. \tag{4}$$

The overall objective function for the generator is summarized as:

$$\min_\Theta \mathbb{E}_{x \sim p_x(x)}[(D_\Phi(G_\Theta(x)) - 1)^2] + \lambda L_{cycle}(\Theta), \tag{5}$$

where λ is a weighting factor for the cycle consistency loss. The cycle consistency may not be able to sufficiently regularize the generator as there exist a number of permutations in the target distribution that maintain the cycle consistency but nevertheless exhibit inferior edge sharpness and intensity contrast. Inspired by Lim et al. [9], we resort to unpaired ground-truth images to inform the generator of intensity variations and structural details desired to be reconstructed. We adapt the generator architecture from [9], i.e., a three-level 3D U-Net [1] with 4 input channels, 64 feature maps in the first convolutional layer and doubling the number of feature maps after each of the two max pooling operation to a maximum of 256. Convolutional layers use $3 \times 3 \times 3$ kernels and are followed by instance normalization and LeakyReLU activation. For the upsampling path we use transposed convolutions. As the adversarial loss evaluated on original-size tiles mainly affects the restoration of low-frequency components, one can resort to multi-PatchGAN [5] to reconstruct finer details using patches cropped from the original-size tiles. Accordingly, Eq. (2) and (3) are reformulated as:

$$\min_\Phi \frac{1}{2}\mathbb{E}_{z \sim p_z(z)}[\sum_{j=1}^m (D_{\Phi_j}(f_j(z)) - 1)^2] + \frac{1}{2}\mathbb{E}_{x \sim p_x(x)}[\sum_{j=1}^m D_{\Phi_j}(f_j(G_\Theta(x)))^2],$$

$$\tag{6}$$

$$\min_{\Theta} \mathbb{E}_{\boldsymbol{x} \sim p_{\boldsymbol{x}}(\boldsymbol{x})} [\sum_{j=1}^{m} (D_{\boldsymbol{\Phi}_j}(f_j(G_\Theta(\boldsymbol{x}))) - 1)^2], \tag{7}$$

where m is the number of discriminators with parameters $\boldsymbol{\Phi}_j$, and the function $f_j(\cdot)$ crops patches of the j-th scale from the input image. We tested the configurations $m \in \{1, 2, 3\}$ and found that using two discriminators yielded the best results. All remaining results were obtained with two discriminators applied on original-size tiles (64^3 voxels) and half-size tiles (32^3 voxels). To get rid of the dependence on ground truth images, we also tested a self-supervised variant of the semi-supervised pipeline by removing all loss parts involving unpaired ground truth, *i.e.*, removing the adversarial loss and reducing the network to the dashed region in Fig. 1. To suppress high-frequency artifacts in the generated images of the self-supervised model, an $L2$ gradient loss is employed as additional regularization in Eq. (5) defined as:

$$L_{gradient} = \frac{1}{n} \|\nabla \hat{z}\|_2^2, \tag{8}$$

where n is the number of voxels, and $\nabla \hat{z}$ denotes the gradient of the generated latent image $\hat{z}$.

4   Experiments and Results

4.1   Datasets

Using the data simulation software and measured PSFs provided in [14], we synthesized an isotropic quad-view data set that is reminiscent of early embryonic development. The quad-view setting was chosen as four views are not too memory expensive and provide the network with sufficient information. The data set consists of 140 sample groups, each of which comprises a quadruplet of view images and the associated ground truth. The training, validation and test sets contain 108, 21 and 11 sample groups, respectively. The view and ground truth images are of size $256 \times 256 \times 256$. In the following context, this data set is referred to as embryo data set. Based on 3D images of *C. elegans* after worm body straightening from [11], we simulated a two-view data set resembling the nuclei distribution of *C. elegans* using PSFs provided in [14]. Compared with the embryo data set, the simulated nuclei are more sparsely-distributed and have fewer touching boundaries. This nuclei data set contains 80 sample groups, among which 68 groups are taken as training set, and 12 groups as validation and test set. The raw and ground truth images are of size $140 \times 140 \times 1000$ voxels.

4.2   Existing Methods for Comparison

To evaluate the performance of our proposed multi-view deconvolution and fusion pipelines, we compare it to an uncorrected raw image (View 0°), the

CBIF [15] and the EBMD [14] algorithms. Both methods are the original Fiji plug-in implementations by the respective authors [14,16,18]. The basic form of EBMD was utilized as this variant provided higher accuracy than the variants with type-I or type-II optimization. For the embryo data set, we adopted 48 for the number of iterations and 0.004 for the weighting factor of the Tikhonov regularization [22] as recommended in [14]. In the context of the nuclei data set, the optimal hyperparameters were manually tuned and empirically set to 15 iterations and a weighting factor of 0.1.

Normalized root-mean-square error (NRMSE) [27], peak signal-noise-ratio (PSNR), structural similarity index (SSIM) [26] and the correlation coefficient (CC) were adopted to quantify the image quality of the multi-view deconvolution results. All metrics were evaluated with MATLAB on the test set of each data set. As the deconvolution results from different methods vary in their value range, it is required to normalize the results prior to quantification. We adopted the normalization method by Weigert *et al.* [27], to cope with varying absolute intensity levels of the different methods. To be consistent throughout metric evaluation, we utilized the same percentile-normalized ground-truth images for the evaluation of other metrics. Importantly, we evaluated each metric in two different settings: one with all voxels, and the other one with only the foreground voxels, *i.e.*, only the voxel positions with non-zero intensity values in the normalized ground truth are considered. The rationale is to measure the deconvolution capability of the proposed models in terms of the content of interest since artifacts in the empty background can interfere with the metric evaluation.

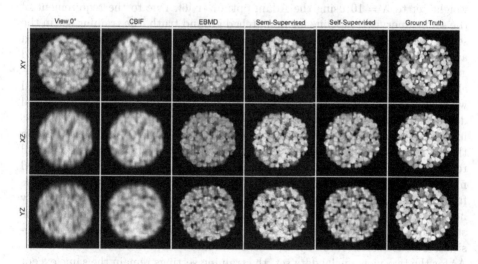

Fig. 2. Deconvolution and fusion quality comparison on the embryo data set. The columns show an uncorrected raw image, the results of the CBIF, EBMD, Semi-Supervised, Self-Supervised methods and the ground truth (left to right).

Table 1. Deconvolution and fusion quality evaluated on the embryo (top) and the nuclei data set (bottom). Left subcolumn: background and foreground, right subcolumn: only foreground.

Methods	NRMSE		PSNR (dB)		SSIM		CC	
View 0°	0.104	0.185	19.685	14.645	0.546	0.845	0.949	0.735
CBIF [15]	0.101	0.181	19.913	14.857	0.508	0.852	0.951	0.749
EBMD [14]	0.078	0.145	22.182	16.763	0.838	0.885	0.971	0.847
Semi-supervised	0.063	0.111	23.998	19.089	0.615	0.913	0.981	0.914
Self-supervised	**0.057**	**0.107**	**24.825**	**19.429**	**0.900**	**0.915**	**0.985**	**0.920**
View 0°	0.084	0.278	21.549	11.151	0.488	0.948	0.862	0.638
CBIF [15]	0.079	0.273	22.050	11.328	0.614	0.950	0.878	0.656
EBMD [14]	**0.079**	0.268	**22.118**	11.460	0.634	0.952	**0.881**	0.670
Semi-supervised	0.087	**0.262**	21.245	**11.655**	0.602	**0.955**	0.852	**0.688**
Self-supervised	0.082	0.276	21.767	11.212	**0.674**	0.954	0.869	0.645

4.3 CNN-Based Multi-View Deconvolution and Fusion

All models were implemented in Pytorch and code is available from https:// github.com/stegmaierj/MultiViewFusion. Given the embryo data set, both the semi- and self-supervised models were trained with input volumes of size $4 \times 64 \times 64 \times 64$, batch size of 1, learning rate of 0.0001, 90 epochs, cycle loss weight set to $\lambda = 10$ using the Adam optimizer [6]. Due to the requirement of the semi-supervised pipeline for unmatched ground truth, the training set in the semi-supervised case was equally divided into two subsets: one half was utilized as inputs to the network while the other half served as provider for unmatched ground truth. The deconvolution and fusion results of the two proposed models are displayed and compared with the existing methods in Fig. 2. Compared with EBMD [14], our methods produce commensurate sharpness and structural details. Furthermore, both proposed pipelines yield stronger brightness contrast in the XY- and XZ-slices and remove more blur in the YZ-slices. Based on the performance metrics listed in Table 1, our methods outperform EBMD [14] regarding both all-voxel and foreground-only evaluations. The semi-supervised model gives an inferior SSIM evaluated on all voxels, which presumably arises from the amplification of noisy voxels in the background due to the intensity normalization in [27]. As SSIM is evaluated in a sliding-window manner it is susceptible to local variations caused by the falsely amplified background intensities. This is corroborated by the SSIM evaluated only with foreground voxels. As for the two-view nuclei data set, the training settings remain the same except for an input volume size of $2 \times 16 \times 128 \times 960$ and training for 500 epochs (other tile sizes like 64^3 and 128^3 consistently performed worse). Similarly, the training set for semi-supervised learning was equally divided into two subsets.

Qualitatively our methods produce deblurring quality slightly superior to EBMD [14] (Fig. 3). However, in the XZ-slices high-frequency artifacts are generated by the GAN-based models. As shown in Fig. 3, the self-supervised model suffers from the high-frequency artifacts in nuclei areas. EBMD [14] outperforms the semi-supervised model for all-voxel evaluation as the proposed model generates artifacts in the dark background, while given only foreground content our method yields the best quality.

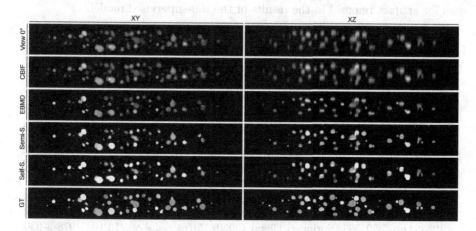

Fig. 3. Deconvolution and fusion quality comparison on the nuclei data set for corresponding XY slices (left column) and XZ slices (right column). The rows show an uncorrected raw image, the results of the CBIF, EBMD, Semi-Supervised, Self-Supervised methods and the ground truth (top to bottom).

5   Conclusions

In this work we approached 3D non-blind multi-view deconvolution and fusion using two CNN-based pipelines on synthetic microscopy data sets. In the quad-view case, both the semi- and self-supervised pipelines outperform the state-of-the-art method EBMD [14] quantitatively and qualitatively in terms of sharpness and crispiness. With respect to the ground truth, the self-supervised model delivered the most reasonable deblurring quality and brightness contrast. Given the two-view data sets, the semi-supervised model surpasses EBMD [14] regarding foreground content while the self-supervised model suffers from the high-frequency artifacts in objects of interest. Consequently, the semi-supervised pipeline is more adaptive in terms of the number of input views and the distribution density of objects of interest. Without using any ground truth, the self-supervised pipeline has demonstrated to be a viable alternative to classical methods. A limitation of the method is that the PSFs are assumed to be known and are kept constant during the training of the GAN. For a more generally applicable method, conditioning the GAN with arbitrary PSFs or performing a blind deconvolution would be interesting next steps. To suppress the high-frequency artifacts, more prior knowledge of the true latent image would be required to regularize the latent image prediction. We intentionally focused on synthetic data in this study that allowed us to quantitatively assess the deconvolution and fusion quality of the different approaches. A logical next step will be to assess how the proposed methods translate to real microscopy images. Moreover, in future work we will also investigate how deeper network architectures, different patch sizes and voxel-shuffle or other upsampling methods can potentially be used for artifact removal in the results of the self-supervised model.

References

1. Çiçek, Ö., Abdulkadir, A., Lienkamp, S.S., Brox, T., Ronneberger, O.: 3D U-Net: learning dense volumetric segmentation from sparse annotation. In: Ourselin, S., Joskowicz, L., Sabuncu, M.R., Unal, G., Wells, W. (eds.) MICCAI 2016. LNCS, vol. 9901, pp. 424–432. Springer, Cham (2016). https://doi.org/10.1007/978-3-319-46723-8_49
2. Chhetri, R.K., Amat, F., Wan, Y., Höckendorf, B., Lemon, W.C., Keller, P.J.: Whole-Animal functional and developmental imaging with isotropic spatial resolution. Nat. Methods 12(12), 1171–1178 (2015)
3. Goncharova, A.S., Honigmann, A., Jug, F., Krull, A.: Improving blind spot denoising for microscopy. In: Bartoli, A., Fusiello, A. (eds.) ECCV 2020. LNCS, vol. 12535, pp. 380–393. Springer, Cham (2020). https://doi.org/10.1007/978-3-030-66415-2_25
4. Huisken, J., Stainier, D.Y.R.: Selective plane illumination microscopy techniques in developmental biology. Development 136(12), 1963–1975 (2009)
5. Isola, P., Zhu, J.-Y., Zhou, T., Efros, A.A.: Image-to-Image translation with conditional adversarial networks. In: Proceedings of the IEEE Conference on Computer Vision and Pattern Recognition, pp. 1125–1134 (2017)
6. Kingma, D.P., Ba, J.: Adam: A Method for Stochastic Optimization. arXiv preprint arXiv:1412.6980 (2014)
7. Krzic, U., Gunther, S., Saunders, T.E., Streichan, S.J., Hufnagel, L.: Multiview light-sheet microscope for rapid in toto imaging. Nat. Methods 9(7), 730–733 (2012)
8. Kupyn, O., Budzan, V., Mykhailych, M., Mishkin, D., Matas, J.: DeblurGAN: blind motion deblurring using conditional adversarial networks. In: Proceedings of the IEEE Conference on Computer Vision and Pattern Recognition, pp. 8183–8192 (2018)
9. Lim, S., Park, H., Lee, S.-E., Chang, S., Sim, B., Ye, J.C.: CycleGAN with a blur kernel for deconvolution microscopy: optimal transport geometry. IEEE Trans. Comput. Imag. 6, 1127–1138 (2020)
10. Lim, S., Ye, J.C.: Blind deconvolution microscopy using cycle consistent CNN with explicit PSF layer. In: Knoll, F., Maier, A., Rueckert, D., Ye, J.C. (eds.) MLMIR 2019. LNCS, vol. 11905, pp. 173–180. Springer, Cham (2019). https://doi.org/10.1007/978-3-030-33843-5_16
11. Long, F., Peng, H., Liu, X., Kim, S.K., Myers, E.: A 3D digital atlas of C. elegans and its application to single-cell analyses. Nat. Methods 6(9), 667–672 (2009)
12. Lucy, L.B.: An iterative technique for the rectification of observed distributions. Astronom. J. 79, 745 (1974)

13. Mao, X., Li, Q., Xie, H., Lau, R.Y.K., Wang, Z., Smolley, S.: Least squares generative adversarial networks. In: Proceedings of the IEEE International Conference on Computer Vision, pp. 2794–2802 (2017)
14. Preibisch, S., et al.: Efficient Bayesian-Based multiview deconvolution. Nat. Methods **11**(6), 645–648 (2014)
15. Preibisch, S., Rohlfing, T., Hasak, M.P., Tomancak, P.: Mosaicing of single plane illumination microscopy images using groupwise registration and fast content-based image fusion. In: Medical Imaging 2008: Image Processing, vol. 6914, p. 69140E. International Society for Optics and Photonics (2008)
16. Preibisch, S., Saalfeld, S., Schindelin, J., Tomancak, P.: Software for bead-based registration of selective plane illumination microscopy data. Nat. Methods **7**(6), 418–419 (2010)
17. Richardson, W.H.: Bayesian-Based iterative method of image restoration. JoSA **62**(1), 55–59 (1972)
18. Schindelin, J., et al.: Fiji: an open-source platform for biological-image analysis. Nat. Methods **9**(7), 676–682 (2012)
19. Schuler, C.J., Burger, C., Harmeling, S., Schölkopf, B.: A machine learning approach for non-blind image deconvolution. In: Proceedings of the IEEE Conference on Computer Vision and Pattern Recognition, pp. 1067–1074 (2013)
20. Schuler, C.J., Hirsch, M., Harmeling, S., Schölkopf, B.: Learning to deblur. IEEE Trans. Pattern Anal. Mach. Intell. **38**(7), 1439–1451 (2015)
21. Son, H., Lee, S.: Fast non-blind deconvolution via regularized residual networks with long/short skip-connections. In: Proceedings of the IEEE International Conference on Computational Photography, pp. 1–10. IEEE (2017)
22. Tihonov, A.N.: Solution of incorrectly formulated problems and the regularization method. Soviet Math. **4**, 1035–1038 (1963)
23. Verveer, P.J., Swoger, J., Pampaloni, F., Greger, K., Marcello, M., Stelzer, E.H.K.: High-Resolution three-dimensional imaging of large specimens with light sheet-based microscopy. Nat. Methods **4**(4), 311–313 (2007)
24. Wang, L., Li, Y., Wang, S.: DeepDeblur: Fast One-Step Blurry Face Images Restoration. arXiv preprint arXiv:1711.09515 (2017)
25. Wang, R., Tao, D.: Training very deep CNNs for general non-blind deconvolution. IEEE Trans. Image Process. **27**(6), 2897–2910 (2018)
26. Wang, Z., Bovik, A.C., Sheikh, H.R., Simoncelli, E.P.: Image quality assessment: from error visibility to structural similarity. IEEE Trans. Image Process. **13**(4), 600–612 (2004)
27. Weigert, M., et al.: Content-Aware image restoration: pushing the limits of fluorescence microscopy. Nat. Methods **15**(12), 1090–1097 (2018)
28. Xu, L., Ren, J.S., Liu, C., Jia, J.: Deep convolutional neural network for image deconvolution. Adv. Neural Inf. Process. Syst. **27**, 1790–1798 (2014)
29. Zhang, J., Pan, J., Lai, W.-S., Lau, R.W.H., Yang, M.-H.: Learning fully convolutional networks for iterative non-blind deconvolution. In: Proceedings of the IEEE Conference on Computer Vision and Pattern Recognition, pp. 3817–3825 (2017)
30. Zhu, J.-Y., Park, T., Isola, P., Efros, A.A.: Unpaired image-to-image translation using cycle-consistent adversarial networks. In: Proceedings of the IEEE International Conference On Computer Vision, pp. 2223–2232 (2017)

Author Index

Printed in the United States
by Baker & Taylor Publisher Services